George Griffith

The aid-de-camp

A Romance of the War

George Griffith

The aid-de-camp
A Romance of the War

ISBN/EAN: 9783337052744

Printed in Europe, USA, Canada, Australia, Japan

Cover: Foto ©ninafisch / pixelio.de

More available books at **www.hansebooks.com**

CHAPTER

...and the evening was... were lit, and the streets were filled with an eager throng hurrying homeward—Baltimore always presents a busy scene at dark, as people of all classes and ages throng its streets, returning from their daily avocations. The merchant and the mechanic, the professional man and the street laborer, the idler and the man of business, the millionaire and the beggar, the sewing girl and the lady of fashion, representatives of all classes, colors and nations under the sun, fill the streets, hurrying on as if their lives depended upon their speed; jostling each other unceremoniously, and filling the air with the sound of their voices. I have often stood upon the street at the hour of twilight, and watched the scene before me with intense interest. One sees human nature in all its forms, on the thoroughfares of Baltimore at this hour.

This evening, the fourth of March, 1861, the streets were more crowded than usual. A dense throng poured through Howard and Liberty streets, into the great highway, Baltimore street, and mingling with the groups already there, filled it to its utmost capacity. The crowd which came in from the Washington Depot, was exceedingly merry, and loud and repeated shouts rose upon the air. There could be heard the shrill nasal twanged voice of the Yankee, and the coarse rough slang of the Western man. Around the Camden street Depot all was bustle and confusion. The large building was black with people, and the long trains, which were constantly arriving from Washington, discharged their passengers and swelled the crowd.

It had been a gala day in Washington, and these people were returning from witnessing the inauguration of Abraham Lincoln to the Presidency of the United States. Fanaticism and sectional hate had suc-

and the greatest Republic upon which the sun ever shone, was tottering to its fall.

Moving on silently and moodily through the throng, as it hurried from the depot, was a young man, whose appearance was so striking that one could not help pausing to notice him. He was of medium height and very slightly framed. He was dressed in a plain suit of black, buttoned closely up to the throat, and he wore carelessly a drab slouched hat. His features were irregular, but striking. There was a firm, grave expression about the mouth, but the keen gray eyes shone with a merry and mischievous twinkle. One felt at a glance that he was far above the average order of men—that he was born for distinction. The gentleman was Mr. Edward Marshall, a young Virginian, who had been for several years a member of the Baltimore Bar. He was twenty-seven years old, and was one of the most distinguished young lawyers of the city. His irreproachable character commanded universal respect, and his influence was very great.

Mr. Marshall had just returned from witnessing the inauguration, and was silently and earnestly reflecting upon what he had seen and heard that day. He passed on with the crowd up Liberty to Baltimore street, and then pausing almost unconsciously, gazed at the throng, as it hurried on, filling the air with its shouts and laughter.

"Aye! laugh on, ye besotted fools," he exclaimed bitterly. "Your fanatical blindness has ruined the country."

He turned away, and was about to continue his walk up Liberty street, when a hand was laid upon his shoulder, and a hearty voice exclaimed:

"Well, Edward, my friend, so you have gotten back. Come with me, and tell me all about the inauguration."

The speaker was an elderly gentleman with a frank, open face, and a cordial, winning air. Mr. Marshall recognized him, and took his hand affectionately.

"You startled me, Mr. Worthington," said he. "I have just returned, and am in no condition to go home with you."

"Nonsense!" said Mr. Worthington, laughing good humoredly, and taking the young man's arm. "Nonsense. You must go with me. Mary will think that the Abolitionists have made off with you, if I don't bring you with me. Come! I will take no excuse."

And the old gentleman bent his steps northward, leading the young man, who seemed to follow very willingly in spite of his alleged unfitness to do so. After a little twisting and turning, they reached Cathedral street, and paused before a large mansion. They ascended the was thrown open. A pair of soft white arms were twined around his neck, his lips were pressed by a dainty little mouth, and a musical voice murmured:

"Welcome, Papa! How naughty to stay out so late."

"There! there!" cried Mr. Worthington, laughingly, as he returned the salute, and passed into the hall, "don't choke me, Mary. Here's a young rascal behind me, who is waiting to come in for his share."

The young lady blushed, and turned to Mr. Marshall, who was standing by the door, which he had closed.

"I did not see you before," she said, holding out her hand.

The old gentleman passed into the parlor, but the young people lingered in the hall. When they entered the parlor there was a bright color on Miss Worthington's cheeks and a happy smile played around Mr. Marshall's lips.

A bright fire was burning in the grate, and by it, in a comfortable arm chair, Mrs. Worthington was sitting. She greeted the young man very cordially. Mr. Worthington had seated himself by his wife, and had drawn a paper from his pocket, and was unfolding it, while he held his feet to the fire.

"Now, sir," said he, turning to Marshall; "make yourself as agreeable as possible to the ladies, while I look over my 'Herald.' Remember, not a word about what you saw in Washington until after supper."

He then opened his paper, and was soon busily engaged in poring over the long black columns of news.

Mr. Worthington was a firm believer in the "New York Herald." His uniform good temper was seriously ruffled, and his enjoyment of his supper greatly disturbed, if he failed to receive it in time to peruse it before tea. After the cares and business of the day were over, it was his chief delight to seat himself by the side of his wife and read the "Herald" until supper was ready. "That Herald" interfered with many of Mrs. Worthington's plans for pleasant chit-chats with her husband before tea. I think there are many wives in the South who are thankful that there is no longer a "Herald" to call their liege lords' attention away from themselves, and who remember it only as an unwelcome visitor.

Mr. Marshall, whether in obedience to Mr. Worthington's injunction, or the dictates of his own heart, I know not, turned his attention to the ladies, and soon a very sprightly and interesting conversation sprang up between them. Mr. Worthington would occasionally look up and join in it for a moment, and then would he again be wrapped up in the contents of his paper.

group. He was Mr. Charles Worthington, the only son and heir of Mr. Nicholas Worthington. He was a young man of twenty-two or twenty-three years of age, and in all respects worthy of the name he bore.

After supper a visitor came in—Mr. William Harris, one of the most prominent citizens of Baltimore.

When the family and their guests were seated around the parlor fire, Mr. Harris exclaimed abruptly, turning to his host:

"Well, Worthington, we are in for it. King Abe is crowned and throned at last."

"Yes," replied Mr. Worthington, smiling. "But I do not envy him."

"Wait six months and you will envy him less;" said Mr. Harris, gloomily. "There is only one course left for us to pursue—the Border States must secede, and cast their lot with their Southern sisters."

"But Lincoln may be more conservative than you now anticipate," said Mr. Worthington, who was unwilling to give up the Union, while a hope of preserving it remained.

Mr. Harris was a thorough Secessionist. He shook his head incredulously, and then asked:

"Have you heard anything from the Inaugural?"

"Marshall heard it," said Mr. Worthington, turning to the young man. "Come, Edward," he added, "give us an account of what you saw and he heard."

All eyes were turned upon Mr. Marshall, who began quietly:

"I went over to Washington last night, in order to avoid the crowd, which I knew would be on the the trains this morning. I spent the night with a friend—and this morning went out upon the street very early. The first thing that attracted my attention was a company of soldiers stationed on the Avenue. I walked on and saw another detachment, and finally discovered that there was scarcely a square of the street that was not guarded by United States Regulars. The tops of houses along the Avenue were lined with riflemen, and detachments of artillery were stationed at various points throughout the city. Happening to know the officer in command of one of these detachments, I approached him, and asked the cause of this extraordinary display of force. He told me that fears were entertained of an attack on the city, or an attempt to assassinate the President elect. General Scott had deemed it best to prepare for the worst. It seems that the officials feared that they would not be able to inaugurate Lincoln without the presence of Federal bayonets. Once, during the day, I was standing by General Scott, who was constantly receiving messages from all parts of the city; and I heard him exclaim, in a tone of great relief:

"Everything is going on peaceably—thank God Almighty for it."

"The old reprobate," exclaimed Mr. Harris, vehemently. "But pardon me for interrupting you. Go on."

"The Inauguration passed off quietly. Lincoln was escorted to the Capitol by a strong guard of cavalry, and was surrounded by troops during the Inaugural ceremony. The whole affair wore an aspect of force which was painful, and I am afraid it was indicative of the future policy of the new Administration."

"But what of the Inaugural? What did he say?" asked Mr. Harris, impatiently.

"I hardly know how to answer you, sir," replied Marshall, hesitatingly. "The Address was so ambiguous and unsatisfactory that I am sure no two persons will construe it alike. He said that he will take care that the laws are faithfully executed in *all* the States. He added, that in doing this there will be no occasion for bloodshed or strife, unless it shall be forced upon the national authority. He will hold the forts, and places belonging to the Government, and he will collect the revenue. I confess that I do not like his address. I think it is intended to deceive and trick the South. I think he means to try to force the seceded States back into the Union."

Mr. Harris smiled scornfully, and Mr. Worthington gazed earnestly into the fire, while Marshall continued:

"As for myself, I have been greatly influenced by it. All of my doubts have been dispelled. What I have this day seen and heard in Washington, has made me a thorough Secessionist."

"Good! I like that!" cried Mr. Harris, seizing his hand.

"I fear that you are right," said Mr. Worthington, sadly. "But God knows that my love for the South is not weakened by my devotion to the Union. I love them both, and never desire to see them separated if it can be avoided."

"But it cannot be avoided, my dear friend," said Mr. Harris. "You must be one of us. Your true place is among the Southern-rights men of Maryland."

"Wait," replied his host; "and if I am more fully convinced of that, I will go over to you. But not now." Then turning to Marshall, he asked, "Who are in the Cabinet?"

"Seward is Secretary of State, and Chase of the Treasury—the others I do not remember."

"Seward and Chase—bad men, bad men," exclaimed Mr. Worthington, shaking his head disapprovingly. "I am afraid they mean war."

"Yes, and a bitter war, too," said Mr. Harris. "But tell me," he tioners, and what did they say of the condition of affairs?"

"I saw Mr. Forsythe this morning. He says that he and Mr. Crawford will wait for a few days before presenting their credentials, in order to give the new administration time to complete its necessary arrangements. He seems to anticipate some trouble, and fears that the Federal Government will not recognise the claims of his Government to independence. I have not seen him since the Inauguration, but I am sure that Lincoln's address must have strengthened his fears."

There was a pause. Suddenly Mr. Harris asked:

"What will Virginia do?"

"Leave the Union, sir, as soon as she is satisfied that it is her duty to do so," replied Marshall.

"If she were out, Maryland could go at once," said Mr. Harris, musingly. "I would give worlds if Maryland had a Governor who could be trusted."

"But surely, Harris, Governor Hicks is a true man," said Mr. Worthington.

"I do not think so," replied Mr. Harris, firmly. "He refuses to convene the Legislature, because that body will summon a Convention and he does not believe that the people desire it. He knows this to be false. From all parts of the State the people are demanding a Convention, and he is daily importuned to allow us to hold one. No, sir he knows that we are for the South, and he has us in his power. But for the injury that it would do the cause, I would propose hanging Hicks to-morrow."

"You are too violent," said Mr. Worthington, with a sigh.

Mr. Harris was an ardent Southern-rights man. He felt the justice of the Southern cause, he knew the popular sympathy with the South that existed in Maryland, and he was anxious that the people should have an opportunity of expressing their will. He felt outraged by, and indignant at the conduct of the Governor, which was slowly but surely betraying the State into the hands of the Federal Government.

Mr. Worthington was one of those conditional Union men who were then to be met with all over the South. He loved the South, and he felt deeply the wrongs that had been done to it; but he loved the Union also, and he did not wish to see it destroyed while a hope remained of the South receiving justice in it. Failing in his efforts to save the Union, he was for immediate and final alliance with the Confederate States.

Mr. Marshall had been a conservative Southern man. He had justified the course of the Southern States, while he had not been averse to a re-construction of the Union. But now Lincoln's inaugural had made him an unconditional Secessionist. The ladies had been silent, but not uninterested listeners to the foregoing conversation. Soon it turned upon other subjects, and in a short time Mr. Harris took his leave. Young Mr. Worthington had an engagement, and Mr. and Mrs. Worthington took their departure from the parlor, and the young people were left alone.

Miss Mary Worthington was, like most of the women of Baltimore, small and beautifully formed. She was a lovely girl, with a fair and smiling face, and large and merry blue eyes. She was only twenty years old. She had been engaged to Marshall for six months, and in six months more she was to become his wife. She was a noble, whole-souled girl, and she was proud of her choice. Well might she have been so. There were few men in Baltimore more worthy, in every respect, of a woman's love than Edward Marshall.

It is not my purpose to make public what passed between the lovers after the old folks left the parlor. I have no right to do so. Such scenes should be kept sacred from prying eyes. Though privileged to remain, and hear and see all that occurred, I know that a third party is always in the way in such cases. Therefore I will follow the example of the old folks, and will retire and close the door behind me

CHAPTER II.

I OPENED this narration with incidents which occurred on the evening succeeding the inauguration of Abraham Lincoln for purposes of convenience. The position and the condition of the country are too well known to the reader to require more than a brief review of them.

The secession of the State of South Carolina had severed the bonds of the Union, and, one by one, the other Cotton States had followed her example, until seven States which embodied the great agricultural wealth of the country, had gone out fr m the Union. These States had confederated in a new Government, had created a new nation, and had assumed all the rights and privileges of an independent Government. The Confederate States had begun their career with a flattering prospect for success Commissioners had been sent to Europe to obtain from Foreign Powers the recognition of their independence and separate nationality. Other Commmissioners had been sent to Washington to treat with the Federal Government upon terms compatible with the dignity and interests of both nations. It was the sincere desire of the new Government to avoid hostilities with the old, and the Commissioners who had been sent to Washington were empowered to treat with the old Government upon the most liberal and honorable terms. From all parts of the country the Federal Government was urged to receive and treat with the Commissioners, who reached Washington about the first of March.

The Confederate Government had been formed during the administration of President Buchanan. The United States pursued a weak and vacillating course. Mr. Buchanan seemed embarrassed. His position was certainly trying, and it would have been well for the country had an abler and a better man filled it.

When the State of South Carolina seceded, the United States held Forts Moultrie and Sumter in the harbor of Charleston. A pledge was given by the United States Government that its military status in that State should not be changed. The State then refrained from making any hostile demonstration upon the Federal forces who held its principal harbor.

On Christmas day, Major Robert Anderson, the commandant of the rest their suspicions of foul play, if indeed they entertained any. On the night of the 26th of December, 1860, he evacuated Fort Moultrie and threw himself into Fort Sumter, an unfinished work, but one of great strength, built on an artificial island in the harbor. He set fire to the work that he evacuated, spiked its guns, and removed everything that he could transport to Fort Sumter. The next day—the 27th—this was discovered, and Fort Moultrie and Castle Pinckney were seized and occupied by the State troops. The fire was extinguished at Fort Moultrie, and soon afterwards the damage was repaired and the Fort made stronger than ever. It was expected that the conduct of Major Anderson, which was in direct violation of the pledge given by the United States would be disapproved by his Government; but Mr. Buchanan not only refused to order him to return to Fort Moultrie, but approved his conduct and sustained him in it.

Warned by this breach of faith, the State of South Carolina seized upon all the property of the Federal Government within its limits, causing a strict account of it to be taken, in order that at the proper time a settlement might be made with the Federal Government. The surrender of Fort Sumter was demanded; the demand being refused, the State collected troops in the harbor, and proceeded to make other preparations to reduce the hostile position. After the formation of the Confederacy the troops were transferred to the Confederate Government, and the works extended. The command was conferred upon Brigadier General Beauregard of the Confederate army. After the occupation of Fort Sumter by Major Anderson, his Government was desirous of supplying him with provisions and ammunition and of reinforcing the garrison with fresh troops. South Carolina very properly refused her consent to this, and the Federal Government resolved to relieve the Fort at all hazards. In January the steamer "Star of the West" was sent to the relief of Major Anderson, but was driven back by the South Carolina batteries.

The only places in the Confederate States held by Federal troops were Forts Sumter and Pickens—the former in Charleston harbor, the latter on Santa Rosa Island in Pensacola Bay, Florida. The troops assembled for the reduction of the latter Fort were commanded by Brigadier General Bragg.

The administration of Mr. Buchanan had been urged to evacuate these Forts, and thus remove all cause for hostilities. This the President declined doing, but gave a pledge that the United States would do nothing to bring about a collision between the opposing forces, if the South would not force it upon them. Had he withdrawn his troops from the Southern forts, he would have removed the great evil which momentarily threatened to bring about a war: and it is possible that the war might have been averted. But he had not the moral courage to do this. He was afraid to brave the storm which such a course would have raised for the time in the North; so he contented himself with promising to refrain from inaugurating any hostile measures, if the Southern States would do likewise. He doubtless hoped to throw all the weight and responsibility of the matter upon the incoming Administration. The Border Slave States had held aloof from their more Southern sisters. They sympathized deeply with them, but wished to exhaust all remedies before leaving the Union. Already they had tried one expedient—the Peace Congress—and this, owing to Northern obstinacy, had proved to be a failure. They were looking about them for some new remedy. Such was the condition of affairs when Lincoln went into power. The country was quivering with the agonies of dismemberment. The new President had it in his power, by pursuing a wise and prudent course, to avoid a war, and to restore harmony to a great degree to the country. He had only to evacuate the Forts, listen to the proposals of the Confederate Commissioners, and if they were compatible with the dignity and interest of his country, to entertain them favorably, and to treat with the new nation upon terms of amity and good will. Such a course would have involved no sacrifice of dignity or interest upon the part of the Federal Government. The history of the times will support me in this assertion.

The Commissioners from the Confederate States arrived in Washington about the first of March. After waiting a few days, in order to allow the new Administration time to complete the necessary arrangements which would occupy its time upon its first entrance to power, they addressed a letter to the Hon. William H. Seward, Secretary of State, setting forth the objects of their mission, and requesting an interview with President Lincoln. Mr. Seward did not receive them officially, but promised a reply at his earliest convenience, and encouraged them to hope that peace and good will might prevail between the two nations, and that the objects of their mission would be successful. He delayed his answer. Judge Campbell, of the Supreme Court of the United States, consented to act as a medium of communication between the Commissioners and Mr. Seward. On the 15th of March Mr. Seward assured Justice Campbell that he felt sure that Fort Sumter would be evacuated "within the next five days," and that "no measure changing the existing *status* prejudicially to the Southern Confederate States," was then contemplated. Thus the Commissioners were amused and detained, while the Federal Government was working silently, but rapidly. The five days passed away, but the Fort was not evacuated. Throughout the North extensive military and naval preparations were begun and carried on with great energy. They attracted the attention and excited the alarm of the Commissioners. Justice Campbell mentioned this alarm to Mr. Seward, and received from him the following answer: "Faith as to Sumter fully kept; *wait and see.*" This was the 7th of April. On the same day, a large fleet, with troops and military supplies, sailed from New York for the South. On the 8th of April, Governor Pickens, of South Carolina, was informed that Fort Sumter would be reinforced and provisioned at all hazards. This information, together with the answer of the Federal Secretary of State, *dated nearly a month back*, declining to receive or treat with them, was conveyed to the Commissioners after the message had been sent to the Governor of South Carolina. The perfidy of the Federal Government was fully evident, even to the dullest comprehension, and the Commissioners immediately took their departure from Washington.

Having anticipated events somewhat, I must now go back for a brief period. Mr. Marshall had watched the course of events with an anxious eye. He feared that war was inevitable. He distrusted the protestations of Lincoln and his Cabinet.

The extraordinary military preparations at the North alarmed him seriously. He saw at once that they were destined for the relief of Fort Sumter. They could not be meant for anything else, for there was no occasion for them elsewhere. Early in April he found it necessary for him to visit Charleston, whither business of importance called him. After parting with his friends, and promising a speedy return, he set out on his journey. He had been furnished by prominent citizens of Maryland with letters to Governor Pickens and General Beauregard, and other distinguished persons in South Carolina. He reached Washington on the morning of the 6th of April.

Among his friends there, was an old gentleman, who had long enjoyed the confidence of those high in authority, and nearly every President, irrespective of party, sought his advice and confidence. He was known to be a strong friend to the South, and had passed unnoticed by President Lincoln. For that individual, Mr. Wheeler, for such was the old gentleman's name, entertained the most thorough contempt.

Marshall never passed through Washington without stopping to see Mr. Wheeler. This time he hurried to visit him, intending to go over to Alexandria in the afternoon, and take the evening train for Richmond. He found Mr. Wheeler at home, and when he told him of his intended visit to Charleston, the old gentleman's countenance wore a look of interest.

"Can I trust you with a secret that may involve the destiny of a nation?" he asked earnestly.

Marshall was surprised, but replied quietly:

"You can, sir."

"I have lived in Washington for a long time," said the old man earnestly, "and I have seen the Government conducted by all sorts of men; I have seen much to make me feel disgusted with, and ashamed of my country, but I have never seen or heard of such villainy as the present Administration is carrying on. All the plans of Lincoln and his Cabinet are known to me."

"I was under the impression that you had nothing to do with the Administration, sir," said Marshall, in great surprise.

"You are right," replied Mr. Wheeler gravely—"But in spite of this all their plans are known to me. I will tell you by what means. Remember, you are not to breathe this to a living soul. When Martin Van Buren was President, unprincipled and treacherous, though he was, he repeatedly sought my advice, I knew all his plans and State secrets, and my advice repeatedly save the country from trouble which his rashness was about to cause it. He had a secret passage made, leading to the chamber in which the meetings of the Cabinet are held, and communicated the secret to no one but myself and a third party, who has since died. No one else knows of the existence of this passage. I was frequently placed in it by Van Buren to overhear the discussions of his Cabinet, in order that I might be the better enabled to advise him. Buchanan did not know of the existence of the passage, and Lincoln does not, I am sure. He has not brains enough to discover it, and no one could tell him of it. Since the entrance of the new Administration upon its duties, I have distrusted it. I have used the secret passage, and have overheard the discussions of the Cabinet. They mean war upon the South."

"I was sure of it," exclaimed Marshall quickly. Then he added, earnestly, "But, my dear sir, you have surely informed the Confederate Government of what you have discovered."

"Alas! no! that is my misfortune," replied his friend. "When I was made acquainted with the passage by Van Buren, I swore a solemn oath never to reveal any thing that I discovered by means of it, at any time. My oath is still binding, and I cannot warn my friends. I know of no man in this city whom I could trust. I have full confidence in you, and what I want you to do is to go with me to-night and take your station in the secret passage. To-night there will be a meeting of the Cabinet, in which a matter of great importance will be discussed. I cannot tell you what it is. You must discover it for yourself, and then hasten to Montgomery and lay the whole matter before President Davis. The Cabinet will meet at nine o'clock to-night. Will you go with me?"

Marshall paused for a moment in deep thought. He was amazed by what Mr. Wheeler had told him. He hardly knew whether to go or not. But the thought of the good he might be able to do for the South, determined him, and he answered firmly:

"I will go with you."

"Very good," said Mr. Wheeler, with satisfaction. "Be here tonight at seven o'clock. We will start a little before eight, in order that we may be in time. You are a lawyer, and have seen much of human nature; but I will show you to-night something that will startle you."

Mr. Wheeler spoke with savage bitterness, and then abruptly changed the conversation. In a short time Marshall took his leave.

During the remainder of the day he wandered listlessly about the city, thinking of what Mr. Wheeler had told him. It was so strange that he could hardly believe it. For a moment he feared that it was some plot to entrap him. But this could not be so; for why should Mr. Wheeler wish to do him any harm? That gentleman had always been noted for his devotion to the South, as well as his unwavering integrity. Strange as the story appeared, it must be true. Besides gratifying his curiosity, Marshall would learn much that would be of importance to the South, and he would dare anything to gain this information.

Taking the precaution to arm himself, he returned to Mr. Wheeler's precisely at seven o'clock that night. He found his friend waiting for him. The old gentleman insisted upon his taking supper with him.

"You will have enough to excite you in what you will see and hear to-night, and I want you to have your head clear and cool, and your mind at rest to begin with. A full stomach and a clear head are inseparable companions."

About eight o'clock they left Mr. Wheeler's residence, and proceeded leisurely in the direction of the White House. Upon arriving at the extension of the Treasury building, they left the Avenue, and entered the President's grounds, and in a few minutes they were standing in the rear of the White House. Glancing hastily around to assure himself that no one was near, Mr. Wheeler approached the house, and drawing from his pocket a piece of steel, pressed it against the wall. Instantly a small concealed door swung around upon a pivot, and the two men disappeared through it, when it was immediately closed. As the door closed behind them, Marshall found himself in a narrow passage and in total darkness. His friend grasped his hand and bade him remove his shoes, be silent and follow him. They passed on swiftly in the darkness, the young man being led by his friend, sometimes turning abruptly and at others ascending long flights of stairs. The atmosphere of the passage was close and confined, and quite cold. Suddenly his friend paused. The air was warmer, and Marshall felt that one of the walls that closed the passage was quite hot. Mr. Wheeler placed his mouth to the young man's ear, and whispered:

"We are now standing in a small chamber constructed in the chimney of the room in which the Cabinet holds its meetings. We can hear the slightest sound that comes from there. I will listen, but I want you to see as well as hear. Remember! whatever you see or hear, you must be silent. Now, look!" So saying he removed the covering from a small opening in the wall through which a brilliant gleam of light came, and moving aside placed the young man at it.

Marshall placed his eye to the aperture, and gazed into the Cabinet council room. He perceived that he was standing some distance above the floor of the room, and could look down upon all that passed within it.

The room was of medium size, and simply but elegantly furnished. In the centre was a large table covered with papers. Seven or eight large arm chairs and a sofa completed the furniture.

Seated in one of these chairs, with his feet thrown carelessly upon the table, with a cigar thrust between his lips, was a tall, dark-complexioned man, with heavy black whiskers. He was dressed in a plain suit of black, which but imperfectly hid the natural ungainliness of his form. His whole appearance was expressive of great awkwardness, and there was about him an air of restraint, which impressed the gazer painfully. There was a dejected and careworn look upon his countenance, and an eager, uneasy gleam in his dark eyes. He was Abraham Lincoln, President of the United States.

Mr. Lincoln was busily engaged in reading a manuscript, which seemed to interest him very much. He was sitting with his face to the fire, and Marshall had an excellent opportunity to study his countenance. He could hardly believe that the awkward and ungainly man before him, whose appearance was at once suggestive of fraud and ignorance, could indeed be the Ruler of the American Republic. He searched his features closely, but nowhere could he discover the evidences of the genius, intellect or wisdom necessary to enable him to conduct the Ship of State safely through the dark waves which were swelling and surging around her. The more he looked at the man before him the more he became satisfied that he had been chosen only that he might be a weak tool in the hands of the wicked rulers of his party. Marshall became interested in his contemplation of Lincoln, and time passed rapidly away. Suddenly the President laid down the papers with a sigh of relief, and glanced at his watch. "Five minutes to nine," he exclaimed, "I did not know it was so late." Then gazing at the pile of papers on the table, he muttered: "Here's a pretty night's work, d—n the luck; I wish I had never been elected; but I must stick to it. Seward says we must run the machine as we found her, if we *bust* her; and I'll do it."

Mr. Lincoln's manner was so strikingly ludicrous that Marshall could scarcely restrain his laughter.

The President then threw himself back in his chair, and smoked in silence. In a few minutes the door opened, and three men entered. Mr. Lincoln rose and greeted them with an awkward familiarity, and requested them to be seated. They were Gideon Welles, Secretary of the Navy; Montgomery Blair; Postmaster General, and Salmon P. Chase, Secretary of the Treasury.

Welles would have been passed by at any time with a mere glance, for there was nothing striking or remarkable in his appearance.

Chase was a fair specimen of a keen, shrewd Yankee sharper. The quick, piercing eye, the restless and uneasy air, the mocking and sinister mouth, all told of trickery and deceit.

Blair was dark and gloomy. A bitter and malignant expression constantly hovered upon his countenance. His keen, observant eye was upon every thing around him, and not a look, not an expression escaped his notice. His manner towards the President was a strange mixture of fawning servility and contemptuous hate.

The three gentlemen had scarcely taken their seats when the door again opened, and Mr. Caleb B. Smith, Secretary of the Interior, entered. He saluted those present with great dignity, and took the seat to which the President pointed.

The door was again opened, and a tall, fine looking man, with a florid face and hair slightly tinged with gray, entered. There was something decidedly striking in this man's appearance. There was an air of defiant boldness and accomplished knavery which at once convinced the gazer that the man was a great villain. There was about him a sternness and haughtiness which agreed well with his manly and dignified figure. He was Simon Cameron, Secretary of War. He was greeted with marked respect by all present, and returned their salutations most courteously.

"All here, gentlemen?" he asked, glancing around the group. "No! where is Governor Seward?"

"Drunk, I guess," said the President, with a laugh, in which all joined. "That reminds me of a joke," he continued. Suddenly he paused. The door was again opened, and this time there entered a man who, having been once seen, is not easily forgotten. He was a small, thin man, with a slight stoop in the shoulders. His hair was gray, and lay in graceful confusion around his brow. He was dressed in a neat and tasteful suit of gray. Every motion was graceful and dignified, and his whole manner was expressive of quiet consciousness of power. But what most interested the gazer was the calm, cold face, in which not a particle of color was visible; the keen, gray eye, which seemed to be reading one's very soul, and the firm, grave mouth, with its expression of energy and power. There was something fascinating in his appearance, but it was the fascination of the serpent, that made the gazer shudder as he looked upon him. One felt that he was a man utterly destitute of principle and integrity, that ambition was his God, and that he feared nothing, scrupled at nothing, in his efforts to gratify his absorbing passion. He was William H. Seward, Secretary of State.

When he entered the council chamber the laughter was hushed, and the Cabinet rose and received him with profound respect. The President glanced at him uneasily, fearing that he had heard his remark, and greeted him with awkward defference. Chase turned away to hide the broad grin which overspread his features; Cameron bit his lip to conceal the ironical smile that hovered around his mouth; and Blair looked on with an expression of withering contempt. Mr. Seward returned the greeting of the President and Cabinet with quiet dignity, and passing on to the table, began to look over the papers upon it.

"Pardon me, Your Excellency," he said, turning to the President, and speaking in a tone of seeming defference, but which an attentive listener might have interpreted as a command, "we are wasting time. There is much to be done to-night, and we had better proceed at once to business."

The President seated himself at the head of the table, and the members of the Cabinet took their places around it; Mr. Seward being on the right and Mr. Cameron on the left of the President.

All eyes were turned to the Secretary of State, and it was easy to see that he was the master spirit of the Cabinet, the true Ruler of the Union.

"Gentlemen," he began, in a calm, clear voice, "we have met to-night to finish the Fort Sumter business. I am informed by the Secretaries of War and the Navy that the Expedition, which has been preparing, for so long, in the North, is at last ready, and will sail from New York in the morning, unless the President shall order otherwise. The chief purpose for which we are assembled to-night is to advise

His Excellency, either to allow the Expedition to sail, or to countermand the order. Our decision is to be final. As for myself, I shall urge him to allow the fleet to sail."

Mr. Welles had listened attentively.

"The position of the Government is very peculiar," he remarked. "If we evacuate Fort Sumter we will create a terrible storm of indignant opposition at home, which will overwhelm us. If we can, by any means, induce the Confederates to attack the Fort, the Government will be safe. We can throw all the odium upon them, and we can so manage the excitement and indignation of the North as to bring on a war, which will result in the utter extermination of slavery."

"If the Expedition sails to-morrow, when will it reach Charleston?" asked Mr. Blair, addressing the Secretary of the Navy.

"On the eleventh of this month," was the reply.

"Now I understand you," resumed Mr. Blair, after a pause. "Your plan is to —"

"Allow me to state it for you," said Mr. Seward, courteously. Mr. Blair bowed and the Secretary of State continued:

"A strong Military and Naval Expedition will sail to-morrow morning, and will reach Charleston on the eleventh of this month. A messenger has already been dispatched to Governor Pickens, to inform him that Fort Sumter will be provisioned at all hazards. He will receive this message on the eighth, the day after to-morrow. It is certain that the Southerners will attack Fort Sumter. That work cannot be held. A few days' bombardment will reduce it. The sailing of our fleet will give the appearance that we mean to save the garrison, when in reality we do not, as I shall soon show you. The fall of the Fort will arouse the Northern and Western States, and we will be able to mould them as we will. It is necessary to sacrifice the garrison of Fort Sumter for the effect that it will have upon the Free States. As soon as we hear of the fall of the Fort, the President will issue his proclamation, denouncing the Southerners as *rebels*, and commanding them to lay down their arms, and disperse within a given time. He will at the same time call for troops to put down the Rebellion. Of course the Southerners will resist, and then we shall have the war in earnest."

"War is a terrible thing," said Mr. Chase, musingly, "and it is a pity to embroil this country in it."

"Then we must go out of power, sir," said Mr. Seward, sharply. "We must either force the South into a war, or we must comply with their demands. We can drag the people into a war, and give them no time to think of anything else; but if we yield to the South, the people will drag us from power. There is a strong anti-slavery sentiment in the country, which will sustain us in a war with the South, and we can work upon the Unionism of the people. There is no retreat for us, gentlemen," he continued emphatically. "We are pledged to carry on the war against slavery, and we have tried the ballot-box long enough We must now use the sword."

"Anderson don't like the idea of relieving Fort Sumter," said the President, raising his head from his hand on which he had been resting it. "He says it's a breach of the faith we have pledged to the South."

"Anderson is a fool," said Seward, contemptuously. "He is too punctilious. But the chances are decidedly against his ever getting out of his Fort. The more martyrs that there are, the more successful will be the cause. To endear Anderson's memory to our people, we'll make a saint of him, by allowing Beauregard to *cannonize* him."

"I see but one difficulty about this war," said Mr. Lincoln, musingly. "It may drive out the Border States, and then we shall have our hands full."

"We are prepared for that," said the Secretary of War. "We wish to force the Border States out of the Union. We have not calculated upon any trifling struggle. We anticipate a long and bloody war; one that will probably last during our entire Administration. But we must deceive the people by prophesying a short war. We will say that we will be able to crush the rebellion in ninety days. We can speedily organize an army. The nine Governors who have just gone from the city, have promised us as many troops as we need. To keep up the deception, we will call for seventy-five thousand men to serve for three months. After this we will be in a position to call for troops for years instead of months, and we shall get as many as we call for. The war will be long and bloody, but it will be advantageous to us as individuals, and in the end we will conquer the South. We have greater resources, more men and material, and we shall finally hold the Southern States as conquered Provinces."

"I care not for the Border States," said Mr. Seward coldly. "I am ready for either the Cotton or the Border States."

"That reminds me of a joke, Seward," said the President, throwing himself back in the chair. "When I was cap'n of a flat boat, I used to hear tell of a man that lived down on the Chesapeake Bay, during the war of 1812. He used to sleep with his rifle at the head of his bed, so as to be ready for the British when they landed. One night there was a terrible thunder storm, and his wife woke him, crying, 'Wake up, husband! the day of judgment has come, or the British have landed.' 'Let 'em come,' cried the old man, jumping up and seizing his rifle—'Let 'em come—I'm ready for either.' So you, Seward, are like the old man; you are ready for either.''

The President sank back in his chair, and laughed heartily at his own joke, inappropriate and stale as it was.

The members of the Cabinet joined in his merriment. A smile of sarcastic contempt played around the lips of the Secretary of State, and he exchanged a meaning glance with the Postmaster General. Then they joined in the laughter.

"Gentlemen," said Mr. Seward, when the mirth had subsided, " we must come to some conclusion upon this matter. What say you? Shall we have a war with the South, or a war with our own people?"

"A war with the South," was the unanimous response.

"Very good," exclaimed the Premier, in a tone of satisfaction. "The President will order the Expedition for the relief of Fort Sumter to sail at once. When the war is begun," he added, turning to the Secretary of War, "we will leave the management of the military details to yourself and General Scott, who has kindly offered to continue to command the armies of the Union. Now that this business is settled, we have other matters to arrange."

Other business was then brought forward and discussed. The Council broke up about twelve o'clock. When the rest of the Cabinet departed, the Secretary of State remained behind.

"Mr. President," said he, fixing his cold, clear eyes upon Lincoln, "you are too faint hearted. You have put your foot upon the plough, and you must not turn back."

"I know that, Seward," said the President, moving uneasily under the cold, satirical gaze of his master spirit. "But I am afraid we are not doing the right thing."

"I tell you, Lincoln, you are a fool. Of course we are doing a d—d rascally piece of business. But we can't help ourselves. So what good will your grumbling do?"

The President laughed, and drawing Seward's arm through his own, said to him:

"You are getting personal. Come with me, and I'll silence you with a drink. I have some prime old brandy down stairs, if the old woman hasn't hid it, or Bob hasn't drank it."

At the mention of brandy, Mr. Seward's eyes brightened, and he followed the President from the room.

From his place of concealment, Mr. Marshall had heard and seen everything that had transpired in the Council Chamber. He was bewildered by the cold-blooded plan of the Cabinet. He could hardly believe them capable of such villainy, and yet he had heard it from their own lips. He turned to his friend, who was standing quietly behind him, and said hastily:

"Let us begone from here. I want to get out into the fresh air."

They retraced their steps, and in a few minutes were standing in the grounds in the rear of the Mansion. They hurried into the Avenue, and after a rapid walk, during which both were silent, they reached the residence of Mr. Wheeler.

"Now, are you satisfied?" asked the old gentleman, when they were seated in the Library.

"I am," replied Marshall. "I shall hasten to Charleston, and offer my services to General Beauregard. After Fort Sumter is taken, I shall inform the Confederate Government of what I have heard."

Marshall passed the remainder of the night with his friend. The next morning he went over to Alexandria, and took the train for the South.

This was Sunday, the 7th of April. On the same day the Expedition for the relief of Fort Sumter passed out of New York harbor, and sailed Southward.

CHAPTER III.

MARSHALL passed through Richmond without stopping. He was delayed for an entire day in North Carolina, and did not reach Charleston until the night of the 10th of April.

He found the city in commotion. It was agitated by the wildest rumors imaginable. Troops were constantly arriving from the interior for service in the approaching engagement. The determination of the Federal Government had been communicated to Governor Pickens, and it had become very generally known in Charleston that an attack would be made soon upon Fort Sumter.

As soon as Governor Pickens received the message of the Lincoln Government, he communicated the information to General Beauregard, who at once telegraphed it to the Confederate Secretary of War, who instructed him to demand the surrender of the Fort, and in case the demand should be refused, to proceed to reduce it.

It was expected that the fleet sent to the relief of Fort Sumter would reach the harbor on the 11th. In all human probability it would have done so but for a storm, which delayed it some thirty-six hours.

On the 11th of April, 1861, General Beauregard demanded of Major Anderson the surrender of Fort Sumter.

On the day after his arrival in Charleston, Marshall hurried through with his business, and when he had finished it, called upon Governor Pickens.

He was received with great courtesy by that gentleman.

"You visit us at an exciting time, Mr. Marshall," said the Governor. "The next twenty-four hours may witness the opening of the great struggle for our independence."

"I have expected this, Your Excellency," said the young man, "and I have hastened here to offer my services to General Beauregard."

"I thank you for your sympathy, Mr. Marshall," said the Governor, grasping his hand warmly. "General Beauregard will not refuse your offer."

"Will you accompany me to General Beauregard's headquarters, Governor?" asked Marshall. I have some important information to lay before him, and, upon reflection, I think that you ought to hear it."

Governor Pickens seemed surprised, but replied at once:

"I was about to go to headquarters when you were announced. My carriage is at the door, and I shall be glad to take you with me."

The two gentlemen then left the house, and entering the carriage which was in waiting, were driven rapidly to the headquarters of the Confederate commander. They were immediately ushered into General Beauregard's presence.

He was sitting at a table, glancing over some papers, but rose as the gentlemen entered. He was of medium size and well proportioned. He was dressed in the plain blue uniform of a Brigadier General, and was scrupulously neat in his attire. His features were prominent, and indicative of his foreign descent. There was much of benevolence and good humor in the expression of his countenance, and through every action there breathed a quiet dignity which at once won the respect and confidence of all persons. You felt at a glance that he was born a soldier. It was impossible to see him without admiring him, and it was equally impossible to know him without honoring and loving him. Uniting that warm and genial disposition which at once endeared him to all, with that brilliant military genius which has ranked him among the greatest Generals of the age, it is not strange that every Southern soldier's heart should throb with devotion, and his eye glow with pride, when he hears the magic name of Beauregard. It is to him the embodiment of chivalry and patriotism. He greeted Governor Pickens cordially, and that gentleman presented Marshall.

"Is my friend well?" inquired the General, when he had read the letter Marshall had brought from Baltimore. "I am glad to meet you as a friend of his."

Marshall bowed, and replied, that the gentleman was well when he left him.

"Are you busy, General?" asked the Governor.

"Not at present," was the answer. "I have demanded the surrender of Fort Sumter, and am now waiting for Anderson's reply. I was about to send for Your Excellency when you arrived. But why do you ask if I am busy? Do you wish me to do anything for you?"

"No," replied the Governor, "but Mr. Marshall has told me that he desires to lay before you some important information, and he wishes me to hear it."

"Indeed," exclaimed the General, gazing earnestly at the young man. "Then, my dear sir, we must hear him at once. It will be some time before I receive Anderson's reply, and we can listen to Mr. Marshall while waiting for it. Now, Mr. Marshall," he added, placing himself in front of that gentleman, "His Excellency and myself are ready to hear you."

After informing General Beauregard of his original purpose in visiting Charleston, Marshall related all that he had seen and heard in the Cabinet Council at Washington. His auditors listened with grave attention, frequently exchanging glances of intelligence. When he had concluded his narration, Marshall turned to General **Beauregard**, and added:

"Seeing that war is inevitable, General, I desire to do what I can for the South. I will be glad if you will assign me to some duty during the approaching bombardment."

"I will, with pleasure, make you one of my Aides-de-Camp for the the occasion," said General Beauregard, cordially. "The information that you bring is indeed important, Mr. Marshall, and I shall at once lay it before my Government." Then turning to Governor Pickens, he added, "So you see, Your Excellency, that my suspicions were not unfounded."

"I am utterly amazed by what I have heard," said the Governor. "I could not have believed any one capable of such diabolical villainy."

The conversation was continued for some time longer. In about an hour, the Aids who had been sent with the message to Major Anderson, returned with his reply.

"What does he say, General?" asked the Governor, eagerly.

General Beauregard tore open the package, and read aloud as follows:

"HEADQUARTERS, FORT SUMTER, S. C.,
April 11th, 1861.

"GENERAL:

"I have the honor to acknowledge the receipt of your communication demanding the evacuation of this fort; and to say in reply thereto, that it is a demand with which I regret that my sense of honor, and of my obligations to my Government, prevent my compliance.

"Thanking you for the fair, manly and courteous terms proposed, and the high compliment paid me,

"I am, General, very respectfully,

Your obedient servant,

(*Signed,*) ROBERT ANDERSON.
Major U. S. Army commanding."

"Major Anderson desired us to say," said Colonel Chestnut, one of the aids who bore the message, "that they will await the first shot, and if you do not batter them to pieces, they will be starved out in a few days."

General Beauregard's face flushed painfully, and he rose from his seat and paced the room nervously.

"It is painful, gentlemen," said he, "to be compelled to attack a brave man with such fearful odds. Anderson is a brave soldier, and it is a shame that he should be sacrificed by the brutal folly of his Government. But if we do not reduce this fort before the arrival of the fleet, we do not know what mischief our enemies may do us."

He then seated himself at a table and wrote rapidly. When he finished, he handed the paper to an Aid, saying:

"Have this telegraphed to Montgomery immediately, and wait for a reply."

The Aid bowed and retired, and General Beauregard, turning to Governor Pickens, continued:

"I have telegraphed Anderson's reply to the Secretary of War, and have asked for further instructions. I appreciate Anderson's feelings, and do not wish to cause him any harm if I can prevent it. I am sure that the Government is anxious to avoid any effusion of blood."

"I honor you for your generosity, General," said the Governor. "But," he continued, while Mr. Marshall has leisure, would it not be well for him to make a written statement of what he has told us. We can lay it before the Government, and save him the trouble of going to Montgomery."

"A very good idea, indeed," exclaimed the General, and rising from his desk, he requested Marshall to take his seat there, and write the statement. While the young man was engaged in preparing the paper, Governor Pickens and General Beauregard walked to a window which commanded a view of the harbor, and conversed in low tones.

The day wore away. A message was received from Montgomery, instructing General Beauregard to make a final offer to Major Anderson to refrain from any hostile measures, if he (Major A.) would agree to evacuate the Fort within a given time, and in the meanwhile would not open his fire upon the Confederate forces. The message was sent to Major Anderson. It was night when his reply was received. He stated that he would evacuate Fort Sumter by noon of the 1 th inst., if, before that time, he did not receive from his Government controlling instructions or additional supplies.

"It is clear that he relies upon the arrival of the fleet," said General Beauregard. "We have no alternative but to attack him."

At twenty minutes past three o'clock, on the morning of the 12th of April, Major Anderson was notified that the Confederate forces would open their fire upon Fort Sumter in one hour from that time.

During the evening Marshall was made acquainted with the other members of General Beauregard's staff, and several officers of distinction. A little after four o'clock, on the morning of April 12th, 1861,

General Beauregard and his staff ascended the upper room of his headquarters, from which an excellent view of the harbor could be obtained. Marshall folded his arms, and standing by a window, gazed out upon the darkness which enshrouded everything. He had not long to wait.

At twenty minutes after four o'clock two brilliant flashes were seen in the direction of James's Island, and two heavy reports in quick succession, from Fort Johnston, came booming over the water. Five minutes elapsed, and then the gloom in the direction of Fort Moultrie was broken by the fierce flashes which leaped from its ramparts, and the silence was riven by the deep thunder of its heavy guns. Then the batteries at Cummings' Point, and the Floating Battery opened fire, and the hostile fortress seemed enveloped in a circle of flame.

"The war has begun, gentlemen," said General Beauregard, grimly.

They remained at the windows, watching the bombardment with the most intense interest. It was a grand scene. Through the deep twilight of the morning could be dimly discerned the dark outline of Fort Sumter, while from every quarter around it, the Heavens were lit up by the lurid flashes of the Southern guns, and the deafening peals of artillery echoed and resounded heavily over the still waters of the Bay. From Cummings' Point and Fort Johnston, huge shells leapt in a sheet of flame from the heavy mortars, and passing rapidly through the air with a graceful curve, exploded over the ramparts of Fort Sumter.

Marshall watched the scene with a thrilling interest. It fully equalled all that he had ever read or dreamed of the fiery splendors of a bombardment.

The fire of the Southern batteries was maintained with spirit, but Sumter was silent. Marshall was surprised by this, and turning to General Beauregard, asked earnestly:

"Does Anderson mean submission by his silence?"

General Beauregard smiled, and answered quietly:

"No! Anderson is too brave a man to surrender before he is forced to do so. He is reserving his fire until he can see our batteries more distinctly. He has few resources to waste."

As he spoke the sky grew brighter, and Fort Sumter could be seen more distinctly. General Beauregard gazed at it for a moment, and then silently pointed towards it. Marshall gazed in the direction indicated by his commander. From the tall flagstaff of the Fort "the stars and stripes" floating defiantly in the morning breeze, told that the Confederate chieftain judged rightly. Anderson was silent, but not conquered

An hour elapsed, but Major Anderson was still silent. Suddenly two bright sheets of flame darted from the dark embrasures of Fort

Sumter, and the deep thunder of two heavy guns replied to the roar of the attacking batteries. The fire of the Southern guns grew hotter, but the Fort relapsed into its former silence. At every discharge the Southern guns grew more perfect, and soon every battery had the exact range of the Fort, and shot and shell fell rapidly from all quarters upon the doomed fortress.

The day opened gloomily. The sky was over-cast with heavy clouds and threatened rain. The wind howled mournfully over the wide expanse of the Bay, and the dense wreaths of smoke hung like a pall over the scene of conflict. About half-past seven o'clock General Beauregard was watching Sumter through his glass. Suddenly he turned to his Aids, and exclaimed quickly:

"Now, gentlemen, we shall have it. Anderson is working his parapet guns."

Scarcely had he spoken, when the dark sides of the Fort were wreathed in smoke, and a rapid fire was opened upon Cummings' Point and Fort Moultrie. Anderson fired rapidly, and he had obtained the range, with great precision. But his balls glanced harmlessly from the Iron Battery, which was the chief object of his fire, and went splashing and crashing into the marsh beyond it.

A dull, drizzling rain was now falling, and heavy, leaden clouds overspread the sky. Major Anderson continued to work his barbette guns, until the constant explosion of shells around him warned him of the danger of exposing his men out of their casemates, and he then withdrew his gunners from the ramparts.

A little after eight o'clock a message was received at headquarters that a large steamer was seen in the offing. General Beauregard glanced meaningly at Marshall, but said nothing. Later in the day it was reported that two other vessels were in sight.

General Beauregard approached Marshall, and handing him his glass, said:

"Take a boat and go over to Cummings' Point, and see what you can make them out to be, and report to me as soon as possible."

Marshall hastened to the wharf where he procured a boat, and was soon on his way to Cummings' Point. He had to pass directly through the line of fire, and shot and shell flew harmlessly on all sides of him. Upon reaching Morris' Island he procured a horse, and soon arrived at the long range of sand and hills which extend along the beach. Adjusting his glass he placed it to his eyes, and gazed anxiously seaward. Lying in the distance, apparently about four miles from the shore, he saw plainly the dark hulls of four large steamers—two of them evidently men-of-war. He felt sure that these vessels constituted the advance of the expedition for the relief of Fort Sumter. They made no attempt to come in, however, but lay quietly in the offing, watching the fight. Marshall made his observations and hastened back to head-quarters, and made his report.

"Do you think they will come in?" asked the General.

"They are lying in the offing very quietly now, sir," said Marshall, "and do not seem disposed to change their position. Remember," he added in a low tone, "the plan is only to make a show of assistance for Anderson."

"True," said General Beauregard, musingly. "But they may wait until the rest come up, and try to enter the harbor to-night. We must guard against this."

The day wore on. The Confederates continued steadily to pour in their fire upon Sumter, and the Fort to respond. During the day, frequent showers of rain fell, but caused no relaxation on the part of either of the combatants. The Iron Battery was severely injured early in the day, and one of its guns was compelled to remain silent during the remainder of the engagement. Sumter was severely injured by the fatal hail which was showered upon her.

At a few minutes before seven o'clock the fire of the Fort ceased, and soon afterwards the Southern guns grew silent also.

As the firing ceased, General Beauregard approached Marshall, in company with an officer whom he introduced as Lieutenant Dozier.

"I have ordered Lieutenant Dozier," said the General, "to go with Colonel Yates. They will station themselves, with several schooners, near Fort Sumter, and will keep bright fires of pine knots burning all night, to enable us to see any vessels or boats that may attempt to enter the harbor. I wish you to go with them. You will have a rough night, I am afraid, but you will be relieved at daybreak. You will inform me at once of anything unusual that may occur, and will report to me when you come ashore in the morning."

Marshall followed Lieutenant Dozier to the wharf, where he found quite a number of schooners and small sloops collected. They went on board one of them, and the little fleet put off. Marshall was introduced to Colonel Yates and the other officers charged with the duty of lighting the harbor, and was soon made to feel himself quite at home.

"We are going upon a dangerous duty, Mr. Marshall," said Colonel Yates. "We are ordered to station ourselves close to Fort Sumter, and Anderson may at any moment blow us out of the water with one of his heavy guns."

"We must take the chances, sir," said Marshall, coolly.

The little fleet had scarcely put out from the shore before the storm, which had been gathering all day, burst forth in all its fury. The winds shrieked wrathfully over the dark waters of the bay, and the rain fell in torrents from the inky heavens. The waves dashed wildly against the sides of the frail vessels, and tossed them fearfully about. Yet they held their course bravely, and soon reached the position to which they had been ordered. The fires were kindled on their decks, and soon the bright flames of the rich pine-wood were sending their ruddy glare far through the darkness and the storm.

Anxious eyes were turned upon Sumter, whose dark outline was revealed by the red light of the flames. The vessels lay at the mercy of the Federal commander. At any time he might sink them with his heavy guns. Fortunately he did not take advantage of his opportunity, and the Fort remained silent.

Sheltered from the fierce storm in the cabin of the schooner, Marshall entered into conversation with the officers with whom he had been thrown. He was delighted with them. All were true and chivalrous Southern men. Each one expressed keen regret at being compelled to attack the gallant commander and garrison of Fort Sumter. The events of the day were discussed, each person having something new and interesting to relate.

"Did you hear any estimate of our loss before you left headquarters?" asked Colonel Yates, addressing Marshall.

"At the last accounts, we had not lost a man," was the reply.

A murmur of surprise ran around the group.

"It is almost incredible," said Colonel Yates. "Anderson's men are splendid artillerists. I remember an incident that occurred a few weeks ago. Our gunners at the Point Battery had set up a hogshead in the bay for a target, and were firing at it. They fired about twenty shots without hitting it. Suddenly a gun was run out and fired from one of the casemates of Fort Sumter, and in a moment more the pieces of the hogshead were floating about the bay. Anderson had hit it at the first fire. If we have escaped unhurt, we owe it to the special interposition of Providence."

"You are right, sir," said Marshall. "I would like to know if Anderson has suffered any loss."

"I am afraid he has," said Colonel Yates. "Almost every one of our shots took effect. If he has sustained no loss, his escape will be even more miraculous than our own. Of one thing I am sure. If the Yankee vessels attempt to enter the harbor to-night, we shall have bloody work."

"I do not believe that they will attempt to enter the harbor to-night," said Marshall. "They are too well aware of the consequences to venture upon such a desperate undertaking. Besides this, the storm will be an excellent excuse for their remaining outside of the bay."

The conversation was continued until late at night. No signs of the Federal fleet could be seen; and weary with the excitement and fatigue of the previous twenty-four hours, Marshall threw himself down upon a bench in the cabin, and soon fell asleep. The storm continued until nearly morning, when it died away.

During the night the mortar batteries continued to fire shells at regular intervals; and the troops spent the night in repairing and strengthening their works.

Marshall was awakened about daybreak by Lieutenant Dozier, who informed him that it was light, and that the vessels were returning to the city. He sprang up hurriedly and went on deck. The storm had died away, and there was every indication of a clear sunrise. As the vessels reached the wharf, Marshall bade a hurried *adieu* to his friends of the night before, and hastened to General Beauregard's headquarters. As he stepped ashore the sun rose majestically out of the ocean, and his brilliant rays scattered the clouds over the heavens.

From the Southern batteries the effect of the previous day's bombardment upon Sumter were distinctly visible. The parapet walls had been battered away, several breaches had been made in the sides of the fort, and the embrasures were greatly torn and injured, and the roofs of the houses were in ruins. As the troops noticed these effects of their work, loud and enthusiastic cheers rang along the shore, and the guns again commenced their fearful thunder.

Marshall reached General Beauregard's headquarters, and made his report.

"I have just learned that several other vessels have appeared off the harbor," said the General to him; "but they do not seem at all disposed to come in. I believe now that you were right yesterday. This fleet is only for a show of relief. A brave man is to be sacrificed in order to enable the villains who control him to stir up a war." An expression of pain passed over his noble features, and he murmured to himself: "Poor Anderson—poor fellow."

At seven o'clock Sumter re-opened its fire, this time directing a heavy cannonade upon Fort Moultrie, which returned shot for shot. A little before eight o'clock, General Beauregard directed Marshall to take a boat and go down the bay to the Floating Battery. "I have been informed," he continued, "that it was struck several times during the engagement of yesterday, and I am anxious to know whether it is damaged, and to what extent. Obtain from Captain Hamilton a statement of its condition, and report to me as soon as possible."

Marshall hastened to the wharf, where he procured a boat. He seated himself in the bow, and the boat shot out from the shore. After getting fairly out into the bay, the rowers made slow progress. There was a heavy ground swell still agitating the water, and the little boat went slowly over the waves. Her situation was perilous in the extreme. She was between the fire of friends and foes, and any chance shot might strike her. During her passage stirring events transpired.

At eight o'clock Fort Moultrie began to fire hot shot, to set fire to Fort Sumter. At ten minutes after eight a thick, heavy column of black smoke rose slowly from the walls of the hostile fortress, and soon the bright, red flames were seen leaping above the ramparts. Fort Sumter was on fire. Loud and thrilling cheers rang along the shore, and the bombardment now grew hotter and fiercer than ever. The wind was blowing from the west, and driving the smoke across the Fort into the casemates where the gunners were at work, and issuing in dense volumes from the port-holes. Major Anderson now rained a fearful fire upon Fort Moultrie, and the combat between the two forts was terrific.

During all this time the little boat had passed safely through the line of fire, and reached the Floating Battery. Marshall sprang lightly on board of it. Captain Hamilton met him, and he delivered General Beauregard's message and received the Captain's reply.

"Look! Mr. Marshall," cried Captain Hamilton, pointing to Fort Sumter, from which large columns of smoke were rising. "Anderson is behaving splendidly. That smoke must be terrible upon his men, but he fights like a hero yet."

The gunners at the Floating Battery watched with great interest the heroic efforts of Anderson and his men; and as that officer, under these trying circumstances, continued to pour in his fire, one of the men sprang upon a gun, and waving his hat, cried enthusiastically: "Three cheers for Major Anderson!" They were given with a will.

"You see that we can admire bravery even in an enemy," said Captain Hamilton, with a proud smile.

"I am proud to be a witness to such generosity, Captain," said Marshall, grasping his hand. "Your guns have done good work. I must return to headquarters. Farewell, sir."

So saying he returned to his boat, and put back to Charleston.

In a few minutes after he left the Foating Battery, he glanced at the fort. The flames seemed to be abating. He turned to look at Fort Moultrie, when he was startled by a tremendous explosion in the direction of Sumter. He turned and saw a dense cloud of white smoke rising above the ramparts of the fort. A portion of the ammunition had exploded in Fort Sumter, and the flames now sprang up with increased fury. When Marshall reached the shore it seemed that the whole fort was on fire, and he shuddered at the thought that the brave garrison might perish in the flames. He at once repaired to headquarters and reported the condition of the battery.

The flames continued to rage fearfully within the walls of Fort Sumter, and soon the guns were silent. Major Anderson and his men were suffering terribly. The smoke was densely packed in the casemates of the fort, and it was impossible for them to work the guns. Several times they were compelled to lie flat upon their faces in order to escape suffocation. But still the brave garrison held out. At a quarter to one o'clock the United States flag was shot away. General Beauregard now sent Colonels Lee, Pryor, and Miles, in a boat, with offers of assistance, if the garrison should be unable to escape the flames. At the same time a small boat containing Colonel Wigfall, another Aid, put off from Cummings' Point, bearing a flag of truce.

The Federal flag soon re-appeared on the walls. Colonel Wigfall reached the fort, and entered through a port-hole. He assured Major Anderson that he had done his duty as a brave man, and urged him to surrender, to save his men. Major Anderson finally consented, and the stars and stripes were hauled down.

In the meanwhile, seeing that the flames did not abate, General Beauregard ordered Marshall to take a fire-engine and go on a steamer, which was in readiness, to Sumter, and render any assistance which the garrison might need. He did so, and reached the fort just as the surrender was made.

When he entered the fort, he found Colonels Wigfall, Lee, Pryor, Miles, Manning and Chestnut, of General Beauregard's staff, present. Major Anderson was standing with his arms folded, leaning against a broken gun carriage.

His face was pale and careworn, and his head was bent in proud dejection. Near him his officers were standing in silence.

Marshall saluted the party and delivered the orders with which he had been charged.

"Gentlemen," said Colonel Wigfall, turning to the group, "Major Anderson has consented to surrender the fort unconditionally."

Major Anderson raised his head and said, calmly:

"I have done my duty. It is useless to attempt to hold the fort longer. I cannot, and will not, sacrifice my men. General Beauregard will impose the conditions. We must accept what he offers."

He bowed his head in proud resignation. His hearers were deeply touched. They admired his gallant conduct, and sympathized with him in his misfortunes.

"Fear not, sir," said Colonel Wigfall, kindly, "General Beauregard knows how to honor a brave man. You have done your duty nobly, and we admire you for it."

Major Anderson's lips quivered with grateful emotion, and he bowed in silence.

The scene that presented itself within the fort, was one of great interest. The flames were still unextinguished. The walls were blackened by smoke and riddled by shot and shell. Large masses of brick and mortar were scattered through the yard, and fragments of shells lay thickly on all sides. Broken carriages and dismounted guns lay along the shattered ramparts. The barracks were in ruins, and in many places still burning. It seemed as if the spirits of ruin and devastation had been at work in the captured fortress.

Strange to relate, not a man of the garrison had been hurt, and no one was injured among the Confederate troops.

Other officers of General Beauregard's staff having been charged with the duty of arranging the terms of the surrender, Marshall returned to headquarters.

As Colonel Wigfall had promised, General Beauregard allowed Major Anderson to surrender on the most generous terms. He permitted him to depart with all company arms and property, and all private property. He afforded him every facility for the removal of his command, and allowed him to salute the flag that he had so gallantly defended before lowering it.

The steamer Isabel was placed at the service of Major Anderson, and General Beauregard desired Marshall to accompany the boat and see the Major and his command on board of the Federal fleet outside of the harbor.

The next day, (April 14th,) at nine o'clock, Marshall reported to Major Anderson. Arrangements with the commander of the fleet, to remove the garrison, had been made earlier in the morning.

A little before noon Major Anderson and his men marched out of the fort to the tune of "Yankee Doodle," and went on board of the Isabel. They were all in full uniform, and carried their arms. A detachment was then sent to the fort to salute and lower the flag.

When the salute began, Major Anderson was standing on the deck of the Isabel, gazing sadly at the flag which was flying from the ramparts. Marshall approached him and asked: "How many guns will be fired, Major; twenty-one?"

"No," replied Anderson, in a quivering voice; "one hundred, and those are scarcely enough."

The gallant soldier's breast heaved with emotion, and turning away he burst into tears.

At the discharge of the seventeenth gun, a caisson exploded, killing one man and wounding five others of Major Anderson's command. A minister was sent for, and the unfortunate man buried on the spot where he had fallen. A volley was fired over his grave, the flag was lowered, and the garrison was transferred to the Isabel. The moorings were cast off, and the steamer started down the bay. Marshall stood on the deck watching the fort. In a few moments deafening peals of artillery were heard in that direction, accompanied by wild and thrilling cheers from the troops along the shore and the persons on the various kinds of water-craft that lined the harbor. The flags of the Confederate States and the State of South Carolina ascended together and waved proudly in the air.

The Isabel sped rapidly down the bay, and passed out to sea. In about an hour she was alongside of the Powhatan, the flag-ship of the squadron. As the steamer was made fast to the frigate, Major Anderson approached Marshall, and taking his hand, pressed it in silence. He then ascended the side of the ship. Captain Gillis, the commander of the expedition, met him at the gangway, and extended his hand to him. The gallant soldier barely touched it, and immediately turned his back upon him. He felt nothing but contempt for the cowards who had left him to his fate.

He had done his duty. Alas! that he should ever have sullied the proud name that he won at Sumter, by his slavish adhesion to a cause that his better nature must have abhorred.

When Major Anderson's men were safely on board the Powhatan, the Isabel returned to Charleston. As she passed Fort Sumter the crew gave three cheers, which were heartily responded to by the new garrison.

Marshall felt satisfied there would be no further hostilities in the neighborhood of Charleston, and he determined to return home at once. He knew that the war was inevitable, and that it would affect Maryland very seriously, and he was anxious to play his part in whatever should happen there.

He waited on General Beauregard and Governor Pickens, and took leave of them. These gentlemen thanked him cordially for his services, and expressed their best wishes for his future welfare. He returned to his hotel, and the next morning saw him on his way to Maryland.

CHAPTER IV.

THE fall of Fort Sumter created a profound sensation throughout the entire country, both North and South. In the North it kindled the fierce fires of revenge and prepared the public mind for civil war. The Cabinet ministers of President Lincoln were not mistaken in their calculations of its effect upon the North. The anti-slavery element of that section was wrought up to madness by it, and eagerly seized upon it as a pretext for war. The conservative portion viewing the attack as an insult to the nation, and an assault upon its rights, clamored loudly for vengeance. The whole North was in a fever. Reason seemed dethroned, and madness ruled the hour.

The news was received by President Lincoln and his Cabinet with great coolness. They had expected it. The first part of their fiendish programme had succeeded admirably, and the condition of the public mind was favorable to the success of the remainder. Artfully pretending to be alarmed for the safety of " the Union, the Constitution, the Flag, and the Capital," the President, in accordance with the plan already mentioned, on the 15th of April, 1861, issued his proclamation, declaring that combinations of men to resist the execution of the laws existed in the seceded States, too powerful to be resisted by the ordinary civil methods, and he, therefore, called upon the States to furnish a force of seventy-five thousand men to suppress these combinations. He stated that the first service which these troops would be called upon to perform, would be to repossess the forts and other property taken from the United States; and he commanded the persons forming the combinations to which he had referred, to lay down their arms and return to their homes within twenty days from that date. This proclamation would have been simply ridiculous, but for the grave issues which it involved. It was in fact a declaration of war against the South.

In accordance with the plan concerted with the Governors of the Free States, troops were raised instantly. The scum of the North and West was mustered into the Federal regiments. Mobs held possession of all the large cities, compelling all persons suspected of friendship for the South, to bow to their dictates and give proof of their loyalty to the Union. The President and Cabinet artfully kept alive and nourished the flames of Northern wrath. The people were completely blinded, and their Rulers led them where they wished.

In the South the fall of Fort Sumter was hailed as a glorious triumph. The people were aroused by it, and the proclamation of President Lincoln, which followed in quick succession, opened their eyes to a sense of their danger.

The Confederate Government now began to act with energy. President Davis called upon the Provisional Congress to assemble at once; and issued his call for troops for the defence of the country. All over the South it was responded to with spirit. Such an army as that which assembled for the defence of the South, the world never saw before. The Merchant, the Mechanic, the Planter, the Laborer, the Millionaire and the Poor Man, all classes, all ages, contributed liberally to swell its ranks. The learned professions of law, medicine, science, and even divinity yielded up their votaries, and in the ranks of the Confederate army might be found the true worth and nobility of the South.

All eyes were turned to the Border Slave States. They were still in the Union, and had been called upon to furnish troops for the Federal army. Would they do so? The issue was no longer between Union and Secession, but between North and South. The Border States at once refused to aid Lincoln in his unholy war upon the South, and, with the exception of Maryland and Kentucky, inaugurated measures which pointed to their immediate secession, and union with the Confederacy.

Marshall travelled rapidly. He reached Richmond on the evening of the 16th of April. He had business which detained him in Richmond during the next day. He had many friends and relatives in the city; and Virginia being his native State, he felt greatly interested in her action.

The Convention was in secret session on the 17th. The Commissioners which had been sent to Washington, had returned. The course which the Federal Government intended pursuing was plain to all, and Virginia could hesitate no longer.

It was the general impression in Richmond that the State would secede that day. Marshall hurried through with his business, and waited with impatience for the news from the Convention. But it did not come. About dark, he was conversing with some friends, when a gentleman, between Marshall and whom there existed a warm friendship, approached him and drew him aside.

"Can you keep a secret?" he asked.

"I can," was the reply.

"Then I will tell you one. Virginia seceded to-day. There are movements on foot, of vital importance to the State, that render it necessary that this should be kept secret."

"Thank God," exclaimed Marshall, fervently. "But," he continued, "the position of the State is very critical. The Federal Government has a strong force of regulars, and may at any time throw them into Virginia. Its war vessels can come up to this very city, and either lay it in ashes or take it. You are at the mercy of Lincoln, and your action certainly evinces a great amount of moral courage."

"You are right," said his friend, musingly. "But anything was preferable to a union with the North. What does Maryland intend doing?"

"We are in a most unfortunate condition," said Marshall. "The State is divided by a wide Bay, and separated from the South by a deep river. 'Our Governor has refused to convene the Legislature, and we have been deprived of a Convention. We have no legal means of expressing our wishes. Our hearts are with you, but I am afraid that we have been betrayed into the hands of our enemies."

"Revolutionize your State. Force her out," exclaimed his friend, impulsively.

"That is easier said than done," said Marshall. "It is too late now. Mark my prediction. In one week from to-day we will be at the mercy of the troops who will assemble at Washington."

The friends soon after separated. The next morning Marshall continued his journey and reached Baltimore, owing to a delay, late in the night of the 18th of April.

In the meantime the Northern troops had begun to assemble. On the 18th of April a body of four hundred half armed and miserable specimens of humanity from Pennsylvania, calling themselves United States soldiers, passed through Baltimore *en route* for Washington. A large crowd followed them through the streets, yelling and hooting at them, and heaping upon them all manner of abuse. The troops passed rapidly through the city, *protected by a strong escort of the City Police*. Before the departure of the trains for Washington, the troops informed the crowd that there would be a body of men through the city the next day, who would make them "*see sights*" if they interfered with them. As soon as it was known that more troops were to be sent through the city, it was determined by the crowd to dispute their passage. About half past ten o'clock, on the morning of the 19th of April, Marshall was standing in his office door, when a man rushed by pale and breathless. Marshall stopped him and asked:

"What is the matter?"

"The Yankee troops are at the Philadelphia Depot, and are butchering the citizens," was the reply. "I am going for my gun."

Marshall hurried into his office, and seizing his revolver, set off at a run for the President Street Depot.

"The 19th of April—the anniversary of the battle of Lexington," he muttered, as he hurried on. "It is appropriate that the first blood of the war should be shed to-day."

When he reached the intersection of Gay and Pratt streets, he found a large crowd assembled, engaged in obstructing the railroad track.

The excitement of the previous day had been greatly increased by the anouncement that a large body of troops would pass through the city on the 19th. Early in the morning a crowd collected along Pratt street, through which the troops must pass to reach the Camden Station, where they were to take the cars for Washington.

To avoid a repetition of the scenes of the day before, the Railroad Companies proposed to convey the troops through the city in thirty-one cars. About half past ten o'clock the trains reached the President Street Depot. A dense crowd had collected around the building. Cheers for "Jeff Davis" and the "Southern Confederacy," groans for "Lincoln and the Yankees," curses, hootings and hisses arose on all sides from the crowd. The cars were hurried out of the Depot, and horses being quickly attached to them they set off at a gallop through the city. The crowd at the intersection of Gray and Pratt streets, seized what rude materials chance threw in their way, and commenced to barricade the track. Six of the cars broke through, but when the seventh arrived the obstructions were too formidable to be overcome. The remaining cars hastily returned to the Depot from which they had started. A consultation of the officers was now held, and they decided that the troops should march through the city to the Washington cars.

Just before the troops left the cars, a young man, (whose name I regret to be unable to give here,) entered one of them, and in bitter terms reproached the troops for aiding in the war against the South. An officer, with the straps of a captain on his shoulders, sprang to his feet, and pointing to the door, shouted wrathfully:

"Leave the car you infernal scoundrel, or I will fire upon you."

The young man turned to him and answered defiantly:

"You are too cowardly to fire."

The officer drew his sword and cut at him. The young man received the blow on his left hand, and closing with his assailant, threw him heavily to the floor. A private sprang to aid his officer, but a blow from the athletic Southerner laid him beside the prostrate captain.

Wresting the sword and scabbard from the captain, he left the car, unmolested by the Yankees, who sat gazing at him, with open mouths and distended eyes, in mute astonishment. He paused for a moment on the platform, and raising the sword aloft, cried exultantly:

"Hurrah, boys! I've whipped two Yankees."

He sprang into the crowd who received him with shouts of delight. The troops were disembarked, and hastily formed. The Mayor of the city, and the Marshal of Police placed themselves at the head of the column, *while a strong Police force was in attendance to preserve order*. The Mayor and the Marshal sympathized deeply with the South, but they resolved to sacrifice their feelings to preserve order and peace in the city, as their duty required them. The mob shouted to them to come away, but they disregarded the cries and kept their places at the head of the troops. As the column moved off, a Confederate flag was displayed in the crowd, and was greeted with wild and enthusiastic cheers. The street was filled with a fierce and exasperated multitude, which moved rapidly along in order to get in front of the troops. Cries of "kill the d—d Yankees," "no quarter," "down with them," rose fearfully on every side. The soldiers gazed around them with a timid air, and hastened forward. They were frightened. Indeed the scene was enough to appal stouter hearts than theirs.

As the troops passed out of Canton Avenue, they were greeted by a volley of heavy stones thrown from the crowd. Two of the men were struck down instantly, and several were severely injured. In a few minutes they were crossing the Pratt Street Bridge. Here one of them turned and fired his musket into the crowd. Stones now fell in showers upon the Yankees, striking them upon the arms, head and body. They swayed from side to side, dodging the missiles which were hurled upon them. Gay street was reached. The troops were halted, and the sunlight flashed brilliantly along the barrels of the muskets which were levelled at the crowd. For a moment there was a pause, and the crowd swayed backwards with violence. "Fire," rang along the line of troops, and instantly a volley of musketry was discharged into the mob. Several were killed instantly, and others severely wounded. A yell of rage burst from the infuriated multitude. Up to this moment they had used no other weapons but stones. Now revolvers were drawn and discharged at the troops, and stones were literally rained upon them. Hundreds left the crowd, and breaking into the neighboring gun-shops supplied themselves with arms, which they used. A rapid running fire was kept up on both sides—the crowd pressing furiously upon the troops. They were now as far as South street. The troops glanced hastily around them, and then broke into a run. A cheer rose from the crowd. "They are running." "Give it to them," were shouted on all sides. At Calvert street a heavy shower of stones fell upon the frightened Yankees, bringing a number of them to the ground senseless. They were again ordered to fire, but they paid no attention to the command, but increased their speed. The order was repeated and the men brought to a halt. A second volley was fired into the crowd, killing and wounding several citizens. The soldiers then resumed their flight. The crowd now seemed wild with fury, and the troops ran with all speed towards the Washington Depot.

They reached the Depot at last, and crowded pell mell into the cars which had been prepared for them. But the fighting was not yet over. Repeated vollies of stones were hurled at the cars, breaking the windows and panels, and cutting and bruising the troops, who were finally compelled to lie flat upon the floor to protect themselves; and whenever the shower of stones would slacken, they would fire through the windows.

A wild cry now rang along the platform:

"Tear up the track."

The dense crowd poured out of the Depot, and ran along the track for more than a mile. It was impossible to tear up the track, for they were not provided with the means of doing so; but in order to obstruct it, huge logs and stones were thrown upon the rails. A strong Police force followed the mob, and removed the obstructions as fast as they were thrown upon the track. Finally the train, amid curses, groans and execrations, passed out of the city and removed the troops from the scene of danger.

Marshall had followed the crowd throughout the entire riot. He disapproved of mob violence, but he was indignant that Northern hirelings should be carried through Baltimore for the purpose of waging war upon the South. He remained a silent spectator of the affair until the troops turned and fired upon the crowd. Then he could restrain himself no longer. He drew his revolver and fired every barrel at the the troops. He had no more ammunition, and his weapon was now useless. He followed the crowd and used stones during the remainder of the fight. When the Yankees left the Depot, he turned away, and was about to return to his office, when he very unexpectedly met Mr. Worthington.

As his eyes fell upon him, Marshall's first impulse was to laugh. The old gentleman was standing on the Railroad, gazing angrily at the train. His hat was mashed out of shape, his collar and cravat were nearly torn off, his dress was greatly deranged, and his features were red and swollen with passion. He grasped his cane in one hand, and shook it defiantly in the direction of the train, which had disappeared. Marshall approached him with feelings of amused surprise.

"My dear sir," he exclaimed, "what on earth are you doing here?"

"The rascals," said the old gentleman, wrathfully, paying no attention to Marshall. "To dare to pass through a Southern city."

Then turning to him, he exclaimed, with a look of astonishment, "Why, Edward, my boy, I thought you were in Charleston."

"I returned late last night," replied Marshall. "But tell me, Mr. Worthington, what have you been doing?"

"Helping to drive those Yankee dogs out of Baltimore."

The old man's eyes gleamed with patriotic fire. Then he glanced at himself, and taking off his hat, straightened it.

"I am considerably used up," said he, laughing. "But there are no bones broken. Come let's get a carriage and go home."

They left the Depot, and soon procured a carriage and started for home. They were met at the door by Mrs. Worthington and Mary. The ladies were terribly frightened at the sight of Mr. Worthington's disordered attire, but were soon convinced that he had sustained no bodily injury. Mrs. Worthington welcomed Marshall warmly, and the young man passing his arm around Mary's waist, pressed a kiss upon her rosy lips.

"Bravo," cried Mr. Worthington. "None but the brave deserve the fair. We have heard of your gallantry at Fort Sumter, young man. I have behaved like a hero, myself, to-day," he added, laughing, and seizing his wife around the waist, he gave her a hearty kiss.

"Where have you been, and what have you been doing, Nicholas?" asked Mrs. Worthington, blushing, while an expression of amusement stole over her face as she glanced at her husband's dress.

"Fighting the Yankees, my dear," was the reply.

"What has been going on? Do tell us, we are dying of curiosity," said Mary, turning to Marshall.

"There has been a serious fight in the city to-day. The Yankee troops passed through Baltimore, and were attacked by the citizens. Your father and myself were in the fight. But can it be possible that you are ignorant of it?"

"We have been in the house all day, and have heard nothing," said Mrs. Worthington, quietly, and drawing closer to her husband.

"Just like you," said the old gentleman, laughing. "The whole town might burn down and you would know nothing of it, provided this house did not catch fire. But sit down, for I am tired enough; and I will tell you all about it."

Mr. Worthington then related the events of the day, and when he had concluded, turned abruptly to Marshall, and said:

"We have seen the accounts of the fall of Fort Sumter, and your name was mentioned quite flatteringly. You must give us an account of the affair."

Marshall related briefly the events connected with the fall of the Fort. His narration was simple and modest, and when he had finished it, Mr. Worthington rose, and remarking that he must make some change in his dress, left the room. His wife followed him, and Marshall and Mary were left alone.

He led her to a seat beside him, and passing his arm around her waist, drew her head down upon his shoulder.

"Are you glad to see me, after my long absence?" he asked, as he gazed tenderly upon the pure face which was uplifted to his own. Mary raised her eyes to his and smiled, and the young man, bending down, pressed a kiss upon her tempting lips.

"I am deeply grateful that you have been permitted to return to me unhurt," she said, as her eyes grew dark with feeling. "If you had been killed, it would have broken my heart."

Marshall was deeply touched. The young girl had, in these few words, laid bare her heart to him. He trembled at the thought that he might not be worthy of such true, womanly love. A prayer rose silently from his heart that he might make her always as happy as she then was. He drew her closer to him, and passing his hand tenderly over the smooth white brows, said in a low tone:

"It is a great blessing to any man, Mary, to have such a dear little woman to love him as you love me. I hope that I may always deserve it."

They sat together for some time, conversing in those tones which only lovers use, until the entrance of Mr. and Mrs. Worthington recalled them to the outer world around them.

In a short time Mr. Harris entered, and seeing Marshall, advanced and shook hands warmly with him.

"I am indeed glad to see you, Mr. Marshall," he said, cordially. "You have returned just in time. I am now on my way to attend a meeting of the citizens in Monument Square, and I have come to ask Worthington to go with me. You must accompany us."

The ladies, dreading a new danger, urged the gentlemen to remain at home.

"There is no danger to be encountered," said Mr. Harris, smiling. "We are going among friends, and it is necessary that we should determine upon our future course of action."

In a short time the gentlemen left the house, and proceeded towards Monument Square. Upon reaching the Court-House, they were admitted to the yard overlooking the Square, where they found Governor Hicks, Ex-Governor Lowe, Mr. McLean, Mr. Wallis, Mayor Brown, and a number of other distinguished gentlemen. Marshall was well known to these gentlemen, and they had seen the accounts in the newspapers of his conduct at Fort Sumter. All except Governor Hicks, thronged around him, and congratulated him upon his safe return.

"You must speak for us, Marshall," said Judge McLean. Marshall would have declined, but his riends urged him so eagerly, that he consented.

Baltimore was full of wild excitement, and a dense throng occupied the large Square—the place appointed for the meeting. Each man was busily engaged in discussing the affair of the morning, and the hum of voices rose confusedly above the living mass.

At last the meeting was called to order. Speeches were made by Governor Hicks, Ex-Governor Lowe, Mayor Brown, and Mr. Wallis. These gentlemen urged upon the people the necessity of moderation and firmness. Governor Hicks denounced the war, and declared that his right arm should be severed from his body, before it should be raised against a Southern State.

When these gentlemen had concluded, Judge McLean was introduced. He was received with hearty applause, for he was known to be a thorough Southerner. He urged the people to resist the Northern Government, and told them that if it were necessary, the Susquehanna should run red with the blood of their foes. He retired amid tremendous applause.

In a few moments he re-appeared, leading Marshall to the front. There was a pause in the crowd. They did not recognize him.

"My friends," said Judge McLean, "I have the pleasure of presenting to you, Mr. Edward Marshall, a gentleman well known to you as an orator and a citizen, but who has won an additional claim upon your respect and admiration, by his gallant conduct at Fort Sumter."

A loud cheer rose from the crowd, and hats were tossed into the air. So intense was their sympathy with the South, that the mere sight of a man who had participated in the bombardment of Fort Sumter, seemed to thrill them with the wildest delight, and it was some time before the applause subsided. Marshall was gifted with a rare eloquence, and the scene before him stirred his very soul. He spoke clearly, fairly and forcibly. He urged immediate union among themselves and prompt action. He counselled them to avoid dissensions among themselves and separate action. He urged them to defend their city and State to the last.

"Your friends are south of the Potomac," he said, in conclusion, "and your enemies are all around you. Your position is unquestionably one of great danger. But will you shrink from it because it is dangerous? I feel that I am addressing the descendants of that heroic 'Maryland Line' of the first Revolution, who shrank from no danger. I know that the spirit of Smallwood and his gallant band—the men who fought at Camden—animates each heart before me. Oh then, by all the proud memories that cluster around the glorious name of old Maryland—by all your fond hopes for the future—by the memories of your forefathers whose names you would not dishonor—by the thought of your children whom you would not have to blush for your degeneracy, I implore you to stand up like men for the independence and rights of your native State. Defend them with your lives, if necessary, and may the Good Lord give you the victory."

Marshall retired amidst tremendous applause.

It was determined to organize the citizens for the defence of the city.

When the meeting broke up, Marshall was surrounded by his friends. who congratulated him upon his brilliant speech. Later in the day he was approached by Mr. Harris.

"I have good news for you," said that gentleman, joyfully. "Hicks has consented to convene the Legislature."

"It is too late to do any great good," said Marshall gloomily. "Our position is desperate, and I am afraid that we shall be overpowered before the Legislature can assemble."

The excitement continued unabated. The military companies of the city were placed under arms, and the citizens armed and organized as far as possible.

On the night of the 19th of April, Governor Hicks gave orders for the destruction of all the Railroad bridges around the city, to prevent the arrival of any more troops. These orders were executed on the morning of the 20th. Saturday passed away without anything worthy of note occurring.

On Sunday morning the churches of the city were more largely attended than usual. Marshall, in company with Mary, attended Grace Church, as was his custom. The morning passed away quietly. About twelve o'clock the congregation was startled by the loud ringing of alarm bells. It could not be for fire, for they were ringing too violently. In a few minutes a gentleman entered the church and whispered to Marshall:

"The enemy are advancing twenty thousand strong from Cockeys ville. Col. Huger wishes to see you. You will find him at the armory of the Maryland Guards."

Marshall whispered to Mary that she must go home. They left the church, and on the way home he told her the cause of the excitement, and urged her to be calm. Her face flushed for a moment, and then became deathly pale.

"Do your duty," she said, in a low tone. "I will trust to God to bring you back to me in safety."

He left her at the door of Mr. Worthington's residence, and hurried to the quarters of the Maryland Guard. He found the streets thronged with people. The congregations of the various churches had been dismissed, and were hastening home with anxious hearts. Old men and boys hurried along in various directions with weapons of every description. Old men, with hoary hair, tottered along with renewed strength, and eyes gleaming with the awakened fire of youth, clutching determinedly the deadly weapons with which they had provided themselves. Men lined the house-tops ready to fire upon the enemy as soon as they should make their appearance. Loud shouts and the hum of eager voices filled the air, and high above all rose the hoarse clanging of the alarm bells. A large crowd had assembled in Monument Square and around Carroll Hall, where the Maryland Guard were quartered.

Marshall made his way through it, and approached the Hall. He found the Maryland Guard drawn up in front of it. A small man, with hair and moustache slightly tinged with gray, and dressed in a plain blue uniform, was sitting quietly on his horse, before them. He was Col. Huger, formerly a distinguished officer of the United States army, but now in command of the troops assembled for the defence of Baltimore.

Marshall approached him, and introducing himself, told him that he had received his message.

"I was advised to send for you, Mr. Marshall," said Col. Huger, dismounting, and handing his bridle to an Orderly, "because I was told that you possess great influence over these people. They are now," he added, glancing around him with an expression of mingled amusement and anxiety, "nothing but a mob, and with all their great bravery, are in great danger of being defeated by organized troops. I want you to aid me in my efforts to bring some order out of this confusion."

"I will do so with pleasure," replied Marshall, "but I expect we shall find it a difficult task."

Colonel Huger then set about making some preparations for an organized defence of the city. The day wore away, but the excitement continued unabated. Late in the afternoon, information was received that the enemy had halted at Cockeysville, and that they would not advance upon the city. The crowd then dispersed, but the volunteers were kept under arms.

I must now anticipate events, and furnish the reader with an outline of the affairs which transpired after the period of this chapter. This is necessary in order that I may not be compelled to pause in the course of this recital, to relate events of a public nature.

After the 19th of April, the excitement increased throughout Maryland, until the whole State, from Pennsylvania to the Potomac, was thoroughly aroused.

But Maryland was helpless. The refusal of the Governor to convene the Legislature had deprived her of a Convention, and the State was without the means of giving authoritative expression of her will Now, the enemy's troops were collecting upon her borders. Her militia were unorganized, and her volunteer troops were scarcely a handful in number. The State was unarmed and almost destitute of defence. Her principal cities, Baltimore and Annapolis were commanded by strong forts held by the enemy; her Governor was disloyal to her, and a willing instrument of the Federal Government. Her position was highly embarrassing and dangerous. But in spite of this, she was ready and anxious to go out of the Union. Alas! she had no means of doing so.

The destruction of the bridges around Baltimore had prevented the United States troops from passing through that city. In order to remedy this, the Federal Government caused them to be conveyed in steamers from Perryville, at the head of the Bay, to Annapolis. Thence they were marched to Washington, along the line of the Railway. They continued to pour into Washington.

The enemy having possession of the capital of the State, the Legislature met in Frederick City. Had they been united and harmonious, they might have carried the State out of the Union even at that late hour, but, unfortunately, they did not represent the sentiments of the people. They delayed until it was too late to act.

The United States having determined to take military possession of the State, B. F. Butler, a Massachusetts lawyer of slender reputation, who had been made, to the surprise of every one, a Major General of Volunteers, was ordered to occupy it with a strong force. The Federal troops already held Annapolis, and others were stationed between Baltimore and the Pennsylvania line.

On the 10th of May, Butler left the Relay House and entered Baltimore. No resistance was offered. Indeed, any resistance that could have been made would have been idle. The troops were marched to Federal Hill, where they encamped.

Governor Hicks now threw off the mask, and openly embraced the cause of the Lincoln Government. He issued orders for the disarming of the volunteers upon the pretext that the arms were the property of the State. They were collected in an outrageous manner and deposited in Fort McHenry. Maryland was now completely in the power of the enemy, and could make no resistance.

General Butler was not continued long in the command of the State. He was assigned the command at Fortress Monroe in Virginia, and was succeeded by Brigadier General Geo. Cadwallader of Pennsylvania, a conceited coxcomb, whose vanity was equalled only by his unfitness for command.

In the South the Border States had seceded, and had entered the Confederacy. Troops had been stationed at exposed points. Yorktown, Norfolk, Manassas Junction, Harper's Ferry, and other places were held and strengthened. A large and gallant army was being rapidly organized in the Confederacy, and a spirit of stern resistance was everywhere exhibited.

Finding that the State was in the hands of the enemy, with no prospect of relief, numbers of Marylanders crossed over to Virginia and entered the Southern army.

Marshall determined to follow their example, and set about arranging his affairs so that he might be able to go South as soon as possible.

CHAPTER V

MARY Worthington was very beautiful, and was greatly admired by the gentlemen of Baltimore. Although so young, she had been in society for several years. She had been eagerly sought by a number of gentlemen, but their addresses had been kindly, but firmly rejected.

When Edward Marshall sought her love, he did not sue in vain. Her heart was at once and willingly surrendered to him, and she loved him with her whole heart, not only for his noble and manly character, and his high and enviable reputation, but "she loved him because she loved him; because she could not help it."

Since their betrothal they had never been separated for more than a day, until Marshall went to Charleston, and Mary was inexpressibly lonely during his absence.

While Marshall was away, one of her friends gave a large party; and Mary was present. There she met with a gentleman from Philadelphia, whom her hostess presented as Mr. Henry Cameron, one of her most intimate friends. Mary did not like him, but she was forced to treat him politely, and as her hostess had spoken of him as such a dear friend, she felt called upon to treat him with more than ordinary civility.

Mr. Cameron was tall and elegantly formed; very graceful, and quite handsome. His features were dark and perfectly chiselled, his eyes large and brilliant, and his hair, which he wore in the most fashionable style, was as black as night. But there was a foul and sinister expression about the mouth, which made one distrust the man.

Mr. Cameron was a thorough man of the world—rather inclined to be heartless, and it was whispered that he was decidedly unprincipled. His manner towards Mary Worthington was marked by great deference, and he was more attentive to her than he had been to any one for some time.

Mr. Cameron looked upon women chiefly as objects formed for his enjoyment. He passed like the bee among the flowers, from one to another, sipping the sweets that lay upon the surface, but never penetrating to the heart—never dealing with their better and truer natures. Indeed he was too thoroughly a man of the world to care much for the heart and its feelings. When he met with Mary Worthington he felt a stronger emotion than he had ever known before. It could hardly be called love; it was not true love, for Mr. Cameron was incapable of experiencing such a pure emotion. But, at all events, he thought that he loved the young girl, and he knew that his feelings for her were different from any that he had ever experienced for any one else.

With a woman's instinct, Mary was at once aware that Mr. Cameron regarded her with feelings of more than ordinary interest. She regretted this: she was annoyed by it. She could not even like him. She felt that he was a cold and heartless man; and while her love for Marshall prevented Mr. Cameron from having the least prospect of winning her, she could not even bring herself to regard him as a friend. She was placed in an unpleasant position, and was glad when the time came for her to return home. Once in the silence of her own chamber, she ceased to think of Mr. Cameron, and her heart warmed and grew tenderer, as her thoughts turned upon her absent lover, and a prayer went up to God that night that He would guide the wanderer safely on his way.

The next day Mr. Cameron called, and she was forced to see him. He called again the next day, and his visits were repeated daily. When Marshall returned Mary told him of all that had happened, and asked him what she must do.

"Treat him politely, but in such a manner as to convince him of the hopelessness of his case," was the reply.

A few days after this, Mr. Cameron called upon her, and addressed her. She rejected him kindly, but firmly.

"I do not understand your conduct, Miss Worthington," said Mr. Cameron. "You have certainly encouraged me to hope for a favorable answer to my suit."

Mary was indignant that he should so grossly and willfully misunderstand her.

"You are mistaken, sir," she replied, coldly. "I have treated you politely, but never encouragingly. I had hoped that my conduct would have discouraged you."

"Why do you object to me, Miss Worthington?" asked the gentleman, with an air of perplexity. "Surely my wealth and position are equal to your own."

"I have declined your offer, Mr. Cameron, because I do not and cannot love you," said the young lady, with dignity.

"Oh! if that is all," said the young man, with a vanity that was truly ludicrous, "you may overcome that feeling. You will learn to love me, and I promise myself the happiness of hearing a different answer from you, yet."

"Your hope is vain, Mr. Cameron," said Mary, with mingled feelings of amusement and indignation. "If I cannot discourage you in any other way, I must tell you that I am already engaged to another. Surely you will now be silent upon the subject."

Mr. Cameron started, as if he had been stung by a serpent. His face grew crimson, and then as pale as marble. He had not expected this announcement.

"To whom?" he asked, in a low, suppressed tone.

"You have no right to ask that question. It should be sufficient for you to know that I can no longer listen to your addresses," was the reply.

Mr. Cameron was silent. Then he exclaimed, bitterly:

"I see it all now. You love that man Marshall. That tell-tale blush proves that I am right," he continued, gazing at her fixedly—then his eyes flashed, and he cried, excitedly, "But he shall never call you his wife. Mine you must and shall be. I have sworn it by all the powers of Heaven, and I will keep my oath."

The young girl's eyes gleamed indignantly.

"You forget to whom you are speaking, sir," she said proudly, as she rose from her seat. "Leave me."

She pointed to the door. Mr. Cameron turned hurriedly, and moved towards it. Suddenly he paused abruptly, and, after a brief hesitation, returned, and said, respectfully:

"I trust that you will pardon my rudeness, Miss Worthington. I hardly know what I am about. I———." He paused and his breast heaved.

The young girl's indignation gave way to a feeling of pity. Perhaps he was really suffering. So she replied gently:

"I accept your apology, Mr. Cameron; but I think it will be better for both parties that our acquaintance should end here."

"Be it as you will," he said, submissively, "but I trust I carry with me your forgiveness."

"I do forgive you, freely," she exclaimed, earnestly, "and I shall not think of you unkindly."

She held out her hand to him. He took it, bowed low over it, and left the room.

Mr. Cameron was maddened by his failure. He could hardly believe it possible that he, the gay and fascinating man of the world, whose boast it was that no woman could resist his arts, had been rejected by a mere girl. He cursed himself bitterly for his folly, and determined to be revenged upon Miss Worthington for her refusal of him. His apology was a stroke of policy

"This cursed war," said he to himself, "will unsettle everything, and then I shall have a better opportunity of executing my plan." This was the last of April. Mr. Cameron at once returned to Philadelphia. He was an intimate friend of and fit associate for General Cadwallader; and when that officer received his appointment as Brigadier General of Volunteers, he was tendered by him the position of Assistant Adjutant General, on his staff, which he at once accepted.

When General Butler was removed from Baltimore, he was succeeded by General Cadwallader. Captain Cameron came with him.

A few days after his arrival in Baltimore, he called at Mr. Worthington's residence, and sent up his card, with a request to see Miss Mary. In a short time the card was returned to him, with this endorsement:

"Miss Worthington declines to receive Captain Cameron, for reasons which are well known to him; and for the additional reason that she cannot consent to hold any friendly intercourse with an enemy of her country."

He read the card in silence, and passed out of the house.

"She shall repent this," he hissed between his shut teeth as he strode along.

Time passed away. One afternoon, about the last of May, Mary went to visit a friend, living in a distant part of the city. She did not start to return home until quite late. It was growing dark very rapidly, and the lamps were not lit. She hastened on timidly, and turned into a cross street. As she did so, a heavy cloak was thrown over her head, and a pair of stout arms seized her. She felt herself lifted from the ground and borne rapidly along. Her captor entered a carriage, still retaining his grasp upon her, and the vehicle was driven away.

From the moment of her seizure, Mary struggled violently, and as she was placed in the carriage, succeeded in partially removing the covering from her head. She immediately uttered a loud cry for help. Her captor roughly replaced the covering, and as the carriage drove off, said to her sternly:

"It is useless to struggle. You must go with me."

The young girl recognized the voice. It was Captain Cameron's.

Since the day that Mary had refused to see him, Cameron had watched her movements, fully resolved upon his plan of revenge. He had seen her leave her father's house, and had followed her to her friend's. He at once procured a carriage, and sending the driver back to the stable, made his servant—a "white negro," who was as great a rascal as his master—mount the box. When Mary reappeared on the street, he followed her cautiously, and taking advantage of the darkness, seized her, and conveyed her to the carriage.

On that very day Marshall had completed his arrangements, and had determined to go to Virginia in a few days. He had business in the western part of the city that afternoon, and was returning to his office about dark, when he saw a short distance ahead of him a female figure, which at a glance he knew to be Mary's. Wondering what could keep her out on the street so late, he hurried on to overtake her. He had almost caught up with her, when she turned into a cross street, and his foot slipped on a piece of apple peel, and he fell to the ground. When he rose to his feet, he saw her struggling in the arms of a man who was placing her in a carriage. He heard her cry for help, and rushed towards the carriage, but before he reached it, it set off rapidly in an easterly direction. He gave chase to it with all speed. In a few minutes he came up with a hack. Stopping it, he sprang to the box and shouted to the driver, as he pointed to the carriage which was flying before them:

"Two hundred dollars if you will catch that hack."

Stimulated by the prospect of such a liberal reward, the driver lashed his horses furiously and urged them to their greatest speed. They were a pair of noble animals, and they gained rapidly upon the carriage. As they drew near it, Marshall turned to the driver, and said hurriedly:

"There is only one way to stop it. We must run into it. You know who I am. I will give you five hundred dollars, and pay for the damage to your hack, if you will run into that carriage and stop it."

Five hundred dollars seemed almost a fortune to the poor driver. It was a dangerous undertaking that he was asked to perform; but he muttered firmly as he lashed his horses onward:

"All right, sir, I'll do it."

The hack flew on at a fearful rate. It was evident that the driver of the carriage saw that he was pursued, for he lashed his horses to their utmost speed. Both vehicles seemed to fly with the speed of the wind, and the fire flew in flames from the heavy paving stones under their wheels. The pursuers were rapidly gaining upon the pursued. On they came, nearer and nearer, until at last they were side by side. They had crossed the bridge, gone beyond High street, and were now in the wide portion of Baltimore street in Old Town.

"Now," shouted Marshall, "run into them."

There was a crash as the two vehicles came together, and Marshall felt himself hurled violently to the ground. For a few moments he lay stunned. When he recovered his consciousness, he sprang to his feet and gazed wildly around him. His hack was lying helplessly on one side and the driver was standing by his panting horses. But the carriage could nowhere be seen.

"Hope you ain't hurt, Mr. Marshall," said the driver, as he saw him rise. "Only one wheel broke. I'd have helped you up, but I was afraid to leave my horses."

"Where is the carriage?" asked Marshall quickly.

"Gone, sir," said the driver. "'Twas too strong for us. We jarred it mightily, but it went by without breaking."

"Which way did it go?" asked the young man, gazing around him.

"There," said the driver, indicating with his finger the direction which the carriage had taken. "But it's of no use for you to follow it. It has been out of sight for nearly ten minutes."

"You are right," said Marshall, gloomily. "I must set the police upon the track of that man, whoever he is. Come to my office in the morning, and I will pay you what I have promised you."

He then sought the office of the Marshal of Police. He stated his case to him, and the Marshal promised to set the detectives to work to discover where the young lady had been taken. Marshall then went to Mr. Worthington's. He found the old gentleman and his wife anxious and uneasy at the absence of their daughter. Charlie Worthington had gone to the house of Mary's friend to see if she were still there, and accompany her home. Marshall told them what had happened. Their alarm and grief were very great. The night was spent in searching for the young girl, but no trace of her could be discovered.

The next morning Marshall was sitting in his office, waiting for a detective, with whom he was to renew the search. The hackman, whom he had engaged on the previous night, had just left him, and he was sitting with his head bowed upon his hands, indulging in the most painful and gloomy reflections. He heard footsteps in the room, and raised his head. The sight that met his view caused him to spring to his feet in astonishment.

Half a dozen Federal soldiers were standing in the room, resting upon their muskets. Near him Captain Cameron was standing, gazing at him in silence, while a mocking smile played around his lips.

"What does this mean, Captain Cameron?" asked Marshall in astonishment.

"It means that I have come to arrest you," was the cool reply.

"Upon what charge?"

"Treason!" said the captain, sternly.

"I have been guilty of no such crime," exclaimed Marshall, indignantly. "I will not be arrested."

"Mr. Marshall," said the Federal officer, coldly, "I have been ordered by General Cadwallader to arrest and convey you to Fort McHenry. You can probably satisfy him of your innocence. I am prepared to execute my orders, and shall certainly carry you with me."

"You take great precautions to arrest one unarmed man," said Marshall, with a smile of contempt. "I will go with you, sir, and I am sure that I shall satisfy General Cadwallader of the fallacy of this charge."

Marshall accompanied Captain Cameron to the Fort. When they reached it he demanded to be taken before General Cadwallader.

"Follow me, sir," said Captain Cameron. "He is in his office."

Marshall followed him until they came to a door at the side of the court yard of the Fort. Cameron opened it, and stood waiting for Marshall to pass in. The unsuspecting young man did so, and the door was immediately closed with a clang, and 'locked. Marshall rushed to it, and tried to open it, but in vain. It was fast. He heard a loud mocking laugh without, and Cameron's voice exclaimed:

"I have you now, Mr. Marshall. Mary Worthington is in my power I shall marry her to-morrow night. You may as well make up your mind to spend the summer here. Good morning, sir."

Marshall shuddered at the thought that Mary was in the power of such a villain as Cameron. In a moment the whole plan flashed across his mind. Mary was to be forced into a marriage with her abductor, and he had been arrested in order to prevent him from giving her any aid. He rushed to the door, and shook it violently, but he could not open it. The window of the room was strongly barred. He shouted aloud for help. The only reply that he received was a gruff command from a Federal soldier, who happened to be passing, to "be quiet." He was helpless, and his affianced wife was in the power of a villain. He covered his face with his hands, and great tears of bitter agony fell through his fingers.

When the carriage which contained Mary and her captor had fairly started, the covering was removed from her head, and she saw that she was in the arms of an officer of the Federal army. In an instant she knew that her abductor was Captain Cameron. She struggled violently to free herself from him, but he held her with a grasp of iron. Her struggles grew feebler, and finally ceased altogether. She had fainted.

The carriage was driven rapidly across the Falls, and towards the eastern portion of the city. Soon Captain Cameron heard a vehicle approaching quickly behind them, and glancing through the back window, he saw a hack coming after them at full speed. He knew that he was pursued, and he shouted to his servant to drive faster. Soon the vehicles were side by side. Then came the crash as the pursuing hack dashed into his own. The carriage swayed violently to one side, but kept on its course. Its great strength had saved it. Cameron glanced at the hack; and an exclamation of savage joy escaped his lips as he saw it fall heavily to one side. The carriage kept on, and turning down Broadway, passed towards Fell's Point. It paused before a dark and gloomy brick house near the water. The young girl, still insensible, was lifted from the carriage and carried to the house.

When Mary recovered her consciousness, she found herself lying on a lounge in a richly furnished apartment. Captain Cameron was sitting by her, bathing her temples with cold water. She started up, and gazed around her with a bewildered stare. She could hardly believe the scene real.

"Where am I?" she murmured.

"Where you will be respected by friends," said Captain Cameron, advancing to her.

She gazed at him with an expression of fear and loathing, and exclaimed:

"Why have you brought me here? What have I done to you?"

"You have nothing to fear, Miss Worthington," said Captain Cameron, in a soothing tone. "You refused to allow me to visit you, and I have determined to see you. This is why I have brought you here. Listen to me. I love you with a wild and fearful passion. I must and will call you mine. Consent to be my wife, and a minister shall join our hands at once. Then I will restore you to your parents. I can easily obtain their forgiveness. I am wealthy, and, as my wife, your every desire shall be gratified. Will you be my wife?"

Mary had listened to him with astonishment and indignation. When he finished, she drew herself up proudly, and gazed at him with eyes whose scornful fires made him lower his, and gaze uneasily upon the floor.

"You disgrace even the uniform that you wear, craven," she cried, indignantly. "I scorn you."

Cameron's face flushed wrathfully, and he clenched his hand. But he calmed himself, and answered coldly:

"I will leave you to your own reflections. You do not quit this house except as my wife. This house, the servants, all things here, are mine. You will be calmer in the morning, and I will see you then."

He turned on his heel and left the room. Mary saw him depart, and heard him lock the door behind him. Then her courage failed her, and she sank on her knees and wept bitterly. She was a prey to the wildest and most terrible fears. She knew that she was in the power of a man who would not scruple at anything. What could she do to protect herself? Then came thoughts of home and her anxious and grief-stricken parents. Then she thought of Marshall. Poor girl! her sufferings were intense. Bodily anguish she could have endured, but it seemed that this mental torture would drive her mad. She passed a sleepless night. She longed for the morning to come, yet she dreaded its approach, for she knew that she would see her persecutor. At last the day came. A few hours after light, the door was opened. She started up in alarm. It was only a servant, who came to extinguish the gas. He returned soon afterwards; and placed a tempting breakfast upon the table, and then withdrew in silence.

The day wore away, and Mary grew calmer. About noon Captain Cameron made his appearance. There was a flush of triumph upon his face, and he seated himself by the side of the young girl, who rose and walked to the opposite side of the room.

"Have you decided?" he asked, rising and approaching her.

"I have, sir," she replied, shrinking from him.

"And your answer?"

"Is the same that I gave you last night," she said quickly.

"Indeed," said Cameron, insolently. "But perhaps you may change it. I have something to say to you, which may influence your decision. Last night, when I was conveying you here in my carriage, I was pursued by your lover, Edward Marshall. He tried to break my carriage and stop me, but he failed to do so. This morning I arrested him upon the charge of treason, and he is now lying in Fort McHenry. The penalty of the crime is *death*, or imprisonment for life. You can save him if you will. Consent to be my wife, and I will release him. Refuse, and he must pay the penalty."

He paused and gazed searchingly at her. She shrank before him, and shuddered under his glance. Her heart ached at the thought of her lover being in the power of her tormentor. She trembled at the thought of his dying the death of a traitor. Should she refuse to save him? Would it be true love to prefer her own happiness before his life? She was cruelly tempted. Then she asked herself would Marshall desire her to save his life by proving false to him. No! They should be faithful to each other under all circumstances. Death would be more welcome than life upon the conditions offered her. Captain Cameron watched her closely.

"Decide!" he said coldly.

She raised her head, which had been bowed upon her breast.

"I have decided," she replied, calmly and firmly. "Do your worst. I defy you."

"Stubborn," he muttered angrily. Then turning to depart, he added, "To-morrow night, at eight o'clock, I will return and bring with me a minister. If you will consent to be my wife, the ceremony will then be performed. If you do not consent to be mine, fairly, I shall have to use force. *Adieu*," he continued, with a mocking smile. "To-morrow night will see you Mrs. Henry Cameron. I congratulate you upon your good fortune."

He passed out of the room. Mary was bewildered by what she had heard. The clouds seemed gathering darkly around her, and she could nowhere see a ray of hope. The day passed slowly and painfully away, and night came at last.

A servant entered and lit the gas, and removed the breakfast and dinner, which lay upon the table untouched, and then passed out in silence. The night wore on, and Mary heard a distant bell toll the hour of nine. She was growing calmer, but more hopeless. She sank on her knees and began to pray. She felt that she had only one friend who could aid her, and that He was powerful to save even in the darkest hour of trial. She prayed most earnestly, and wrapt in the fervor of devotion, spoke aloud, and was unconscious of what was passing around her.

The door opened silently, and a woman entered so noiselessly that Mary did not hear her. She closed the door softly, and advanced into the room. She was a woman of queenly beauty, with hair as black as jet, and large and lustrous dark eyes. Her closely fitting dress revealed the exquisite proportions of her magnificent form. There was a strange and brilliant glow upon her cheeks, a stern, determined look upon her face, and in her right hand she grasped firmly a large knife, which glittered brilliantly in the gas light.

As she advanced into the room, her eyes fell upon the kneeling form of the young girl, and she paused in astonishment. She leant forward and listened eagerly. Unconscious of her presence, Mary prayed to be delivered from the power of her oppressor. An expression of joy passed over the stranger's features. As the young girl continued, her features grew very pale, and she clasped her hands, and her frame shook with a sudden and violent anguish. The knife fell from her hand, and clattered upon the floor. Roused by this noise, Mary sprang to her feet, and gazed first at the strange woman and then at the knife, in great alarm. In her weak and exhausted condition, the excitement was too great for her. Her features grew ashy pale, she reeled, and would have fallen to the floor, had not the strange woman received her in her arms. She carried the insensible girl to the lounge, which was near, and tried to revive her. She gazed with a pitying expression upon the pure young features, now as pale and rigid as marble.

"It cannot be true," she muttered to herself. "There is no sin here. I must, I will save her."

At last Mary slowly opened her eyes, and fixed them upon the strange woman, who was bending over her with a look of deep and tender sympathy. That look re-assured her, and she rose from the couch, and turning to the stranger, asked in a tremulous voice:

"Who are you, and what do you wish?"

"I am your friend," replied the woman, in a voice of exquisite melody, "and I have come to save you. But first tell me how you came here."

Mary gazed into her face for some time, and meeting again those sad and tender eyes, she felt encouraged, and told her all that had happened to her.

"I knew it," said the stranger, in a tone of relief. "Henry Cameron lied to me."

"Who are you?" asked Mary, almost forgetting her danger, in her admiration of the exquisite beauty of the stranger.

"It is a very long story," said the woman, in a bitter tone, "but I will try to make it as short as possible. I am the daughter of a wealthy merchant of Philadelphia. Henry Cameron won my love, and professed to love me. He persuaded me to consent to a private marriage, for my parents objected to him. We were married, as I thought. When he came to Baltimore with General Cadwallader, I came with him. Four days ago he came to me and told me that our marriage was an imposture—that I am not his wife." The strange woman's breast heaved convulsively, her cheeks grew crimson, and her eyes flashed as she continued rapidly, "I cannot tell you how I suffered, how I implored him to repair the wrong that he had done. He told me that he loved another—that he would bring her here, and marry her this week. Our relations to each other might remain undisturbed, but he was determined to marry another. I grew calm, and seemed to consent to his arrangement, but in my heart I resolved upon a deep and fearful vengeance. I could not lift my hand against *him*, but I resolved that when he brought here the woman that had weaned his love away from me she should not live. When you came, I tried to reach you at once, but failed. To-night I came to take your life. But when I saw you kneeling, and heard you pray to be delivered from this place and its owner, a new light flashed through my mind. Henry Cameron had resolved to make you another victim of his villainy. I see through the whole plot now. That prayer has saved you. God has answered it, and I am now here to rescue you."

"Oh save me!" cried the young girl falling on her knees and seizing the hand of her unknown friend. Save me, and Heaven will bless you."

The woman gazed at her with a strangely sweet expression, and the dark eyes filled with tears.

"Poor child," she murmured, "he must indeed be a villain, who can harbor a thought of evil against you. But fear not. I have promised to save you, and I will do so."

She rose and assisted Mary to put on her bonnet and shawl.

"Now," said she, "give me your hand, and follow me in silence. We have no time to lose. We may be discovered; but we must run the risk."

They left the room and entered a long, dark passage. Mary was led rapidly through it by her unknown friend, and then down a long flight of stairs. Soon they were standing in the street.

The night was clear, and the cool river breeze felt refreshing to the young girl's flushed cheeks. They walked on some distance from the house, and soon turned into a large and wide street. Here her guide paused.

"This is Broadway," she said, as she pressed Mary's hand. "You can find your way home by following the railway into Baltimore street. I must leave you now."

"Surely," exclaimed Mary, in a tone of astonishment, "you are not going back into that villain's power. Come with me. My parents will protect you."

"No," replied the stranger, gazing at her, sadly. "I am not fit to go with you. I have sinned too deeply."

"But you sinned unwittingly," said Mary, as the tears of sympathy came into her eyes. "My parents will love you for the service that you have rendered me. We shall obtain for you the forgiveness of your own parents, and you shall be restored to your home again."

"It cannot be," said the strange woman, mournfully. "Villain as he is, I love Henry Cameron too well to leave him. I feel that my fate is linked with his. I must return. Farewell."

She clasped the young girl in her arms, and pressing a kiss upon her lips, hurried away. Mary stood gazing after her with tear-dimmed eyes, and wondered how a woman so beautiful, and of such a noble nature, could love a man so depraved as Cameron.

A woman's love once won, remains steadfast and faithful forever. Time and changes cannot alter it. It burns purely and brightly amid care and sorrow, coldness and neglect. All things else change, but it remains the same. Woman brought woe into the world by her first sin, and God in pity, planted in her breast that holy love, which has made earth almost an Eden, and without which Heaven itself would seem lonely. From his cradle to his grave, it watches over man with a tender and noble devotion. It guards his infancy, blesses his prime, comforts his age, and cheers his dying hour. It asks nothing but a return of love—that a spark of its own divine fire may enter into and fill the heart beloved, expanding and beautifying it, and encircling man's life with a nobleness and truth that his own nature is powerless to bestow.

Mary watched the stranger until she had passed out of sight. Then she hastened into Baltimore street, and hurried homewards. The streets were almost deserted, though it was not quite eleven o'clock.

She reached her father's house in safety. A light was burning in the hall. She rang the bell, and in a few moments the door was opened, and she was clasped in her brother's arms. He bore her into the parlor where her parents were seated, with sad hearts, for they had despaired of seeing her again. It was a joyful meeting. When all parties grew calm, Mary told of her capture, imprisonment and escape. That night prayers of thankfulness went up to God, and the unknown woman, who had caused all this joy, was not forgotten in them.

As soon as Mr. Worthington had been informed by Marshall of the abduction of his daughter, he searched for her in every direction. On the next morning he went to Marshall's office, to ascertain whether the young man had discovered any trace of the absent one. To his astonishment he learned that Marshall had been arrested and conveyed to Fort McHenry. He immediately procured a carriage, drove to the Fort, and requested permission to see the prisoner. His request was refused, and he was ordered away from the Fort. He returned to the city, and passed the day in searching for his child. He returned home at night, and in answer to his wife's eager inquiries, replied that he had learned nothing. The family were assembled, with sad hearts, and in silence, in the parlor that night, when they were aroused by the ringing of the bell. The surprise that awaited them was joyful beyond description.

The morning after his sister's return, Charlie Worthington went to Fort McHenry, and asked to see Captain Cameron. He was informed that the Captain had left that morning for Philadelphia, and would not be back for a week. He returned home, resolving to await Captain

Cameron's return, when he would make him account to him for his conduct to his sister.

That afternoon Mary glanced over the evening edition of the "American," when her eyes fell upon the following paragraph:

"*Mysterious Affair.*—This morning the body of a female of extraordinary beauty was found floating in the harbor at Fell's Point. Marks of violence were found upon her person, and a deep wound had been inflicted just over the heart. The coroner's jury decided that she came to her death from the effects of a wound inflicted by the hands of some unknown person. Nothing has been discovered which may lead to the detection of the murderer. A deep mystery shrouds the whole affair. Who the unfortunate woman was whose wonderful beauty and sad fate have excited so much sympathy in her behalf, we know not. She was, doubtless, one of those unfortunate beings, whose bitter lives too often close in this tragic manner."

Mary was satisfied that this unfortunate woman was her preserver, who had fallen a victim to Cameron's anger, when he discovered her escape. She shuddered with horror at the thought. But she could not consent to allow her to be buried in the place assigned to such unfortunates for their last, deep sleep, so she urged her father to have the body interred in his own lot in Green Mount. This he readily promised her. But when she urged him to take some steps to have the murderer brought to justice, he replied:

"That I cannot do. We can prove nothing, so we must remain quiet. We shall only get ourselves into trouble by attempting to investigate this matter."

Since her escape, Mary had thought often and anxiously of her lover, languishing in his prison. On this evening she approached her brother, and taking him aside, said to him:

"Charlie, is it possible for me to see Edward?"

"No," replied her brother, "he is not allowed to see any one."

"But I must see him," she continued, earnestly.

"That is impossible," said Charlie, sadly.

"It is not impossible," she replied energetically. "We must try to get him out. I have a plan which I know will succeed. Listen to me, and I will tell it to you."

She spoke rapidly and earnestly, as she related to him a plan, which she had conceived, for Marshall's escape from the Fort. Charlie listened attentively, and when she had finished caught her in his arms, and gave her a hearty kiss.

"By George, Mary," he exclaimed, enthusiastically, "you are worth a thousand such men as I am. I never would have thought of this. I'll do as you say, and we can try it, at all events."

The next afternoon a carriage drove up to Fort McHenry, and a lady and gentleman alighted from it, and asked to see General Cadwallader. They were shown into his presence. The gentleman introduced himself as Mr. Hopkins of Baltimore, and the lady as Miss Marshall.

"Miss Marshall has come, General," said he, to solicit a short interview with her brother, who is now confined in the Fort."

"It cannot be granted, sir," said General Cadwallader, sternly. "State prisoners are not allowed to see any one."

The lady begged earnestly to be allowed to see the prisoner, and after much solicitation General Cadwallader consented to allow her an interview for half an hour. She thanked him warmly, and followed the officer, whom he summoned to conduct her to the cell of the prisoner.

Edward Marshall, since his confinement, had seen no one but a soldier who brought him his meals of bread and water. He was sitting with his face buried in his hands, indulging in the most painful reveries. Suddenly he heard the door open, and some one enter, and then the door was closed. He looked up, and saw a lady gazing at him. He rose to his feet, and in a moment he sprang forward and clasped her in his arms.

"Mary, dear Mary," he exclaimed, in a tone of delight, "this is indeed a welcome visit. But tell me how came you here? Where is Cameron?"

"I must talk quickly," said she, smiling through her tears, "for I have much to tell you, and only half an hour to stay."

Then she told him all that had happened to her since their last meeting.

"Thank God," he murmured, as he drew her closer to him, "you are safe now. I can bear this imprisonment more patiently now. It was indeed kind in you to come here."

"I am here as your sister," said Mary, "and I have come to enable you to escape."

She produced two packages, which she had concealed upon her person.

"These bundles," she continued, "contain a life-preserver, a coil of rope, and a set of burglar's tools. With the last named articles, you can cut away the bars of your window, and escape from this cell. Once out of it, I rely upon your own ingenuity to get out of the Fort. You must go to the river and swim across to the Anne Arundel shore— the bridges are guarded. Charlie and I will wait for you with a horse, about a mile down the Annapolis road, at midnight. You will find in the bundles everything that you need."

"You are a treasure, Mary," cried Marshall, kissing her gratefully.

"Wait until you are out of this place, and then thank me," she said gently.

The half hour passed quickly away. The officer who had conducted her thither, entered the apartment, and informed her that the time had expired.

"Good bye, brother," she said, with a smile, as she rose to go away. Marshall bent over and kissed her, and told her that she must come again. As she reached the door, Mary turned to her lover with a smile of encouragement, and then left the room.

When he was alone, Marshall opened his bundles. In one of them he found a life-preserver, and a coil of rope in the other, a burglar's file, saw and knife, and a small phial of oil. He examined them closely and found them in excellent order. Then he concealed them in his bed, until he should need them.

About nine o'clock an officer entered the room to see if all were safe. Marshall was lying on the bed, pretending to be asleep. The officer flashed the light of the lantern in his face, gazed at him for a few minutes, and then passed out.

When he thought that it was time to begin his work, Marshall removed the crystal from his watch, and felt along the face to ascertain the position of the hands, for it was too dark to see them. As well as he could determine the time in this way, he found that it was almost eleven o'clock. He placed his life-preserver around him, and moved the table quietly to the window. Mounting upon it, he took out his fine burglar's saw and began cutting the bars, using the oil to dampen the metal and prevent any noise being made. He cut away bar after bar, and laid them silently upon the floor, until only one remained. He was some time in accomplishing this, and his heart beat violently, and his breath came quickly, as he worked upon the remaining bar. Suddenly, just as the bar was cut through, his hand slipped and knocked the heavy iron rod out of the window. It fell to the ground with a heavy sound, and Marshall crouched down from the window in alarm. He trembled violently, as he heard the rough challenge of the sentinel on the ramparts just above him:

"Who goes there?"

A cat had been frightened from its place of rest under the window by the fall of the bar, and darted off in the direction of the rampart. Marshall heard, with delight, the sentinel mutter, as he passed on:

"Curse that cat. That's twice to-night it has startled me."

He waited for a few minutes until everything grew quiet. Then he climbed through the window, which was not far from the ground, and let himself drop gently into the yard of the Fort. He crouched in silence for a moment in the shadow of the wall, and gazed around him. Having ascertained the exact position of everything, he crept slowly and stealthily towards the rampart facing the back branch of the Patapsco. He reached it, and then gazed down below him, and around him. Before him and on either side lay the river, with a score of lights twinkling upon it, and reflecting in its clear bosom the millions of stars that were gemming the Heavens. The breeze blew coolly in from the bay, and the waters rippled upon the shore with a low, murmuring sound. Back of him was the city with its dark structures and long rows of lights.

Marshall did not pause long to observe these things, but leaning over the rampart, fastened his rope to one of the long black guns that projected over the wall. He had just made it fast when he heard footsteps approaching. He crouched down in the shadow of the gun-carriage and remained perfectly quiet and motionless. Soon a sentinel approached, and pausing by the gun-carriage, rested his musket on the ground and leaned upon it.

"I wonder what they are doing in old Virginny to-night," he muttered, as he gazed over the river. "By George! I would like to be there."

He stood for several minutes, which seemed to Marshall like ages, and then took up his musket and passed on. Marshall watched him until he was out of sight, and then creeping to the edge of the rampart, seized the rope, and lowered himself quickly to the ground without. He was now free from the Fort, but the danger was not yet passed. As he reached the ground, a wild and joyful sensation passed through his frame; he was a freeman once more, and with God's help he would remain so. He hastened along the shore until he reached a point some distance above the Fort. He was an excellent swimmer, but the river was wide, and the night dark and cold. He removed his clothes and fastened them in a bundle, which he tied to his head. Then inflating his life-preserver, he fastened it around him, and entered the water, which chilled his very blood. He struck out boldly from the shore, and was soon fairly out into the stream. After a considerable length of time he reached the Anne Arundel shore. Here he dressed himself, and glancing at his watch, saw by the clear starlight, that it was two o'clock. He was well acquainted with that portion of the country and was enabled to reach the Annapolis road without delay.

Hastening on, he soon discovered three dusky objects standing in the road some distance ahead of him. He hurried on and discovered that they were three horses which were being held by a man. A woman was standing in the road near them. Marshall advanced to meet her, and she sprang to him with a cry of joy.

"Free, Mary, free, thanks to you, darling," he exclaimed, as he clasped her in his arms.

"I feared that you had failed, you were so late," she said as she clung closely to him. Then she added, "Here is Charlie holding the horses."

Marshall advanced and greeted his friend.

"I must thank you, too," he said, as he grasped Charlie's hand, warmly. "Both of you have proved true friends in the hour of need."

"We have no time for talking, Marshall," said Charlie. Put Mary on her horse, and then mount this one. I went to your room to-day and packed a small portmanteau with some necessary articles. I have strapped it to your saddle. Father found a check with your name to it, in your check book, and he has drawn all your money out of the Bank. Here it is," he added, handing him a heavy pocket book. "In this pocket book you will find a paper with directions for your route, and where to stop. Now let's be off. We will ride a mile or two with you."

Marshall then placed Mary on her horse, and mounted his own. They set off. In about an hour he bade his friends farewell, and they turned back towards Baltimore. He watched them until they were out of sight, and then set off at a gallop.

The first and second days of his journey passed away without the occurrence of anything unusual. On the third day he entered Saint Mary's county. He stopped at a country inn to procure something to eat, about noon. After he had finished his dinner, he sat on the gallery smoking a cigar, and conversing with the landlord, whom he discovered to be a Southern man. Suddenly the latter uttered an exclamation of surprise, and gazed up the road in the direction from which Marshall had come. Marshall gazed in the direction indicated by the landlord, and saw a Federal officer followed by six dragoons, coming down the road.

"It is too late to escape," he said, turning to the landlord. "We must trick them. Go into the house, and if they ask you who I am, say that I am a Government agent, and that I am awaiting an escort of cavalry which I have sent down the road."

The landlord entered the house, and Marshall remained in his seat, smoking with apparent indifference. The Yankee troops approached rapidly and soon reached the inn. They dismounted and fastened their horses, and entered the house. As they passed Marshall, he nodded carelessly to them. They returned his salutation, and gazed searchingly at him.

Approaching the landlord, the officer asked sternly:

"Who is that man in the porch?"

"That man," said the landlord, laughing good humoredly, "is the bitterest Yankee that I ever saw. If you'll take my advice, gentlemen, you'll let him alone. He is a Government agent, or something of the kind, and has come down here to hunt up Secessionists. I heard him talk pretty sharply to a Brigadier General who was here with him about three hours ago. He sent him away somewhere, and is waiting for him now. I wouldn't be surprised if it's Mr. Seward himself."

"Oh, ho!" said the officer, knowingly, "if that's the case, I'll stand around. I heard that there was a Secessionist here, and I came to catch him."

"No," said the landlord, "that gentleman and the General that he's waiting for are all that have been here to-day."

"Then I'll get back to camp," said the officer, and he left the room, followed by his men. As he passed out, he glanced respectfully at Marshall, who was sitting quietly smoking. He rose, and approaching them, asked, with an appearance of interest:

"What is the matter, gentlemen? Is anything wrong?"

"No, sir," replied the officer. "We heard that a Secessionist was here, and we came after him."

"No one has been here since I arrived," said Marshall. "You were misinformed."

"I expect so, sir," said the Lieutanant. "Good day, sir."

He left the porch, followed by his men. They mounted their horses and set off rapidly. Marshall watched them until they were out of sight, and then turning to the landlord, asked, as he broke into a loud laugh:

"Well, landlord, what do you think of that?"

"It was capital," said the host, whose fat sides shook with mirth. "They are the greenest fools that I ever saw."*

Marshall bade adieu to the landlord, and continued his journey towards the Potomac. He reached the river in good time and crossed safely into Virginia.

* The incident related above happened to a friend of the author on his way from Maryland to Virginia in 1861.

After Marshall parted from Mary and her brother, they returned slowly and crossed the Long Bridge about daylight. Mr. and Mrs. Worthington were delighted with the success of Mary's scheme, and the old gentleman, fondly kissing her, called her his little heroine. The evening papers were filled with long accounts of the visit of Marshall's sister to him, and his escape from the Fort. The affair created considerable excitement. Efforts were made to discover Mr. Hopkins and the young lady, but they were unsuccessful.

About three weeks after this, Mr. Worthington was warned by a friend that he would be arrested in a few days by the military authorities. He left Baltimore with his family, and settled in St. Mary's county. Here he was so much annoyed by the enemy's troops that he crossed over to Virginia, and moved to Richmond.

CHAPTER VI.

AFTER he reached Virginia, Marshall hastened to Richmond, and immediately made application for a commission. He received it, and was ordered to report to General Johnston at Harper's Ferry. He at once left Richmond, and soon reached that place. This was the first of June.

A large force had been collected at Harper's Ferry, and placed under the command of Colonel Thomas J. Jackson. On the 23rd of May General Joseph E. Johnston, of the Confederate army, assumed command of the troops assembled there.

Marshall had never seen so large an army before, and the scene was novel and interesting. On the morning after his arrival he rose very early, and walked down to the Railroad Bridge, and paused to survey the scene.

On all sides of him the mountains rose high above him, and through the pass, the Potomac rushed foaming and dashing over its rocky bed, while the quiet "Daughter of the Stars," the romantic Shenandoah, swept gracefully around from her home in the hills, to mingle her peaceful waters with the angry torrent of the lordly Potomac, which seemed to flow gentler and softer after the union. From the lofty heights on the Maryland shore, the dark heavy guns frowned down upon the little village, and the white tents of the army thickly dotted the dark sides of the mountain on every hand. The drums were beating the reveille, and the camps were soon alive with human beings.

During the day Marshall had nothing to do, he crossed to the Maryland shore, and walked up the river some distance, happy to be in Maryland again. He was deeply imbued with a spirit of earnest piety, and the scene around him impressed him powerfully with the majesty and glory of its Creator.

It is difficult to conceive how any one can stand upon the shore of the Potomac at Harper's Ferry, where the mountains are cleft in twain by the mighty river as it foams and dashes over the rocks that seek to impede its way, as if in its wrath it would sweep them from its path, and hear the ceaseless roar of the torrent as it chaunts its sublime hymn of praise to God, and see the grand old mountains lift up their heads to Heaven, everlasting witnesses of the majesty, the power and the goodness of the Almighty, without feeling his heart touched and subdued with reverential awe. Truly God manifests His glory everywhere in His works, but nowhere more strikingly than at this place. The scene may lack that calm beauty which so often captivates the eye, but it is awful in its grandeur and terrible in its sublimity.

Marshall was deeply impressed by the scene. The impulse was powerful, and he could not resist it. He turned into a clump of bushes, and falling on his knees, lifted up his soul in prayer.

As he rose from his knees the bushes parted, and a man stepped from among them. He was rather tall, and broadly and squarely built. His hair was dark and short, and his beard and moustache were closely trimmed. There was a mild, but firm expression upon his face, and his eyes shone with a calm and tranquil light. He was dressed in a plain gray uniform, and the three stars upon his coat collar told that he held the rank of Colonel in the Confederate army. He was a man that one would trust at a glance. One felt from the moment that he saw him that he was of iron will and great genius. He advanced to Marshall, and with a smile, whose wondrous sweetness none could resist, held out his hand to him.

"Pardon me for intruding upon you, sir," he said in a tone of kindly interest, "this is a sight so rarely witnessed here, that I cannot help commending it whenever I see it. My name is Jackson, and I am very glad to meet you. May I ask your name?"

Marshall took his hand, and told him his name. He gazed at him with interest. Colonel Jackson was already well known to the public, and Marshall felt that he was yet to be one of the master spirits of the war.

Colonel Jackson was going to Harper's Ferry, and asked him to accompany him. He questioned him in regard to his position in the army.

"I have not been assigned to any regular duty," said Marshall, "and am now awaiting orders."

"If you do not object," said Colonel Jackson, "I will ask General Johnston to let me have you as an Aid. I am commanding the first Brigade of this army, and I shall need you."

Marshall replied that he would be very glad indeed if such an arrangement could be made. When they reached Harper's Ferry, Colonel Jackson paused, and grasping Marshall's hand, said to him earnestly:

"I was very much gratified by what I saw of you to-day. Continue in the good path you have chosen. Believe me, sir, there is nothing nobler than a Christian soldier. We see too few of them in the army.

We cannot expect God's blessing to rest upon us, if we are forgetful of Him. Continue to pray, and you will always be successful."

He turned away and walked towards General Johnston's headquarters, and Marshall repaired to his tent, to muse over his singular interview. The next day Colonel Jackson sent for him, and told him that General Johnston had assigned him to duty on his staff. Marshall immediately entered upon his duties, and discharged them with ability and faithfulness. Colonel Jackson was always kind and ready to render him any service; but he was silent and reserved in his manner towards him, as he was to every one else. On the day that he became acquainted with Marshall, he was surprised and drawn out of himself by his admiration for the young man's conduct. Now he sank back into his habitual reserve. But this did not mar the natural kindness of his character. A kinder, truer gentleman, a more sincere and humble Christian never lived. Modest and retiring as a girl, brave as a lion in battle, generous to a fault, is it a wonder that his troops love him? Is it strange that they shout for joy until the Heavens ring, whenever they see the old worn cap, and the faded, gray uniform appear? But why write thus? Why attempt to eulogize Jackson? He needs none of this. He has written his name in every Southern soldier's heart.

Time passed away. On the night of the 13th of June, Colonel Jackson informed Marshall that General Johnston had determined to evacuate Harper's Ferry.

"Have everything in readiness to leave at a moment's warning," he added.

On the next day preparations for the evacuation were begun. The heavy guns that could not be removed were rendered unfit for service, and rolled into the river. The splendid railroad bridge was blown up, and the public buildings set on fire. The flames rose rapidly, and were soon hissing and roaring around the tall structures. It was a grand scene. The heat in the village was so intense that the troops could with difficulty perform the work of removing the stores. Thus the day passed away, and at last all was ready. On the 15th of June the army left Harper's Ferry, and marched towards Winchester. On the evening of the same day they encamped about a mile beyond Charlestown.

The town of Harper's Ferry was built upon a neck of land at the confluence of the Potomac and Shenandoah rivers. It was capable, at the time of its occupation by General Johnston, of a successful defence against any force which the enemy could bring against it. But it might be easily converted into a disadvantage to the South. The enemy's troops might invest it at any moment, hold its garrison in check, and command the Valley, or attack General Beauregard in the rear at the Manassas Junction. A strong column of Federal troops, under Major General Patterson, was advancing through Maryland, and General Johnston had held Harper's Ferry, only that he might draw them into Virginia. As soon as this object was accomplished, he evacuated the place and moved towards Winchester.

On the morning after he encamped at Charlestown, he heard that the enemy's advanced brigade, under General Cadwallader, had crossed the Potomac at Williamsport, and was advancing upon Martinsburg. General Johnston immediately wheeled his army to the right, and marched north towards Martinsburg. It now became known among the troops that they were advancing to meet the enemy, and they broke into loud and enthusiastic cheers. The men were raw and unused to the fatigues of a march, but they bore them with patience, and pushed forward cheerfully, urged on by the prospect of a speedy engagement with the hated foe.

General Cadwallader had crossed the Potomac and was advancing into Virginia, as he supposed, to pursue a flying foe, for he had heard of the evacutation of Harper's Ferry. He had scarcely entered Virginia, when he was informed that General Johnston, whom he supposed to be retreating, was advancing to meet him. For a moment the Yankee General was completely nonplussed. Then thinking discretion the better part of valor, he re-crossed the Potomac; and retreated into Maryland, and did not pause until he reached the main body of Patterson's army at Hagerstown.

As soon as General Johnston heard of Cadwallader's retreat, he halted his troops. Then sending Colonel Jackson's Brigade towards Martinsburg, to watch Patterson, and a detachment of his forces, under Colonel A. P. Hill, to occupy Romney and watch McClellan, who was then in Western Virginia, and who he feared might attempt to form a junction with Patterson, General Johnston marched to Winchester.

While engaged in watching Patterson, Colonel Jackson inflicted great damage upon the Baltimore and Ohio Railroad.

On the 3rd of July General Patterson crossed the Potomac and advanced towards Martinsburg. Colonel Jackson broke up his camp near Martinsburg, and marched to meet him.

Arriving near Falling Waters, he found the enemy drawn up in line of battle. He detached from his command the Augusta regiment, (Colonel Harper's) and one six pounder from Pendleton's Battery, in all not quite four hundred men, and advanced towards the enemy.

The Federals consisted of General Cadwallader's Brigade, about 3,000 strong, and a fine battery of artillery. They held a fine position, and it seemed that they would completely envelope the little band that advanced so fearlessly to meet them. Their skirmishers were thrown out in front of them, and as Jackson's men came up, opened a rapid fire upon them. Hastily advancing his skirmishers Colonel Jackson ordered them to open fire upon the enemy. This they did with spirit, compelling the Federal marksmen to retire in confusion to their main line. The Confederate infantry were the hardy mountaineers of Augusta, whose hands had grasped the rifle almost from infancy, and their fire was terribly destructive. The one six pounder gun tore great gaps in the Federal ranks. During the action, Colonel Jackson sent Marshall to Captain Pendleton with orders to fire at a certain point. He delivered the order and remained at the battery to watch the effect of the shot. Captain Pendleton stood grimly by his piece, and sighted it in the direction indicated.

"Ready," he exclaimed, and the order was obeyed. Then raising his eyes to Heaven, he cried earnestly, "May the Lord have mercy upon their poor souls. *Fire.*"

A flash and a roar followed this singular command, and the shell tore fatally through the Federal ranks. The gun was loaded again, and the same prayer and the same command uttered.

Marshall could not help smiling at this singular exhibition of skill and pity. Soon after this he was sent to the front with orders to the skirmishers. As he passed along the line, he glanced at the enemy. At this moment an officer, evidently an Aid, rode down to the Federal skirmishers. There was something very familiar in his appearance, and as he was not far off, Marshall raised his glass and looked at him. He recognised him at once. It was Captain Cameron. He hurried down to the line of skirmishers and delivered his orders. Then approaching one of the men, he asked him to lend him his rifle. The man handed it to him, and Marshall dismounted.

"Now," said he to the man, "if you will hold my horse for a minute, I will try to bring down one Yankee at least."

"All right, sir," said the man, grasping the bridle. "But who do you want to shoot?"

"That officer," replied Marshall, pointing to Cameron. "He is an old acquaintance."

The man laughed, and Marshall raised the rifle to his shoulder, and took deliberate aim at Cameron, who was now sitting on his horse gazing through his glass at the Confederate lines. Marshall was an excellent marksman, and he aimed his rifle slowly and carefully. The distance was not very great. He pressed the trigger, and in an instant Cameron threw up his arms and fell heavily from his horse.

"Good!" shouted the owner of the rifle. "I knew old Joe would reach him. By George, Lieutenant, that's the best shot I ever saw. I believe you have killed him."

As soon as he had fired, Marshall lowered his rifle, and raised his glass to his eyes. He could see the men crowd around Cameron, and raise him from the ground, and carry him to the rear.

"No," he said, as he closed his glass, and placed it in the case. "I saw him place his hand to his breast. He is only wounded."

Thanking the man for the use of his rifle, Marshall mounted his horse, and returned to Colonel Jackson.

The fight continued for nearly an hour longer. Finally, the enemy making an attempt to outflank him, Colonel Jackson withdrew his troops, and retired in the direction of Martinsburg. He had held in check for nearly two hours a force greatly superior to his own, and as he now withdrew, the enemy made no attempt to follow him. He continued his retreat until he reached Darksville, a little village about five or six miles south of Martinsburg. On the same evening he was joined by General Johnston, who had advanced from Winchester with the main body of the army.

The report of Marshall's exploit spread rapidly through the army, and whenever he passed them, the men pointed to him and said:

"There goes the man that made that good shot with Alick Gray's rifle."

On Wednesday, July 5th, General Patterson's army, twenty thousand strong, entered Martinsburg.

General Johnston disposed his troops in order of battle, and awaited the advance of the enemy. But General Patterson was in no hurry to meet him. He preferred remaining at a safe distance. General Johnston waited four days for him, and then finding that the latter did not intend meeting him, retired to Winchester.

At first the troops thought that they were running from the enemy and refused to march, and it required all the persuasive eloquence of General Johnston to induce them to fall back. They did so sullenly and discontentedly, not dreaming how soon their great Commander would lead them to immortal glory.

During the march the men suffered very much. While advancing to meet the enemy, they had not complained, but now when they had no such excitement to encourage them, they flagged and straggled very much.

On the first day of the march Marshall was riding near the Augusta regiment, when he heard some one exclaim:

"I say, Lieutenant!"

He looked around and saw the man whose rifle he had used at Falling Waters. He checked his horse and rode by him.

"I say, Lieutenant," continued the man. "We are not running away from the Yankees; are we?"

"Oh, no!" said Marshall, smiling, "General Johnston has laid a trap for them, and he is now trying to draw them into it. Take him at his word, and wait. You'll have fighting enough before this month is out."

"I'm mighty glad to hear you say that," said the man, his countenance, as well as those of the men who heard the conversation, brightening. "We'd rather die than run. 'Twouldn't do for us to go back to Augusta, and say that we ran away from the Yankees. The gals wouldn't notice us."

Marshall laughed, and replied:

"You need not fear. The girls will be proud of you yet."

"All right, sir," cried a score of voices. "We see how it is now. Old Joe Johnston knows what he's up to."

This conversation, unimportant as it may seem, had a wonderful effect upon the men. It was repeated throughout the brigade with numerous additions and embellishments. It inspired fresh confidence in the Commanding General, and the troops pushed on with more cheerfulness than before. At last Winchester was reached, and the army encamped around the town.

In a day or two Colonel Jackson received an appointment as Brigadier General, as a reward for his services, and especially his conduct at Falling Waters. Marshall was continued as an Aid-de-Camp.

I must now pass rapidly over events. On the 15th of July, Colonel Stuart, commanding the cavalry of the army of the Shenandoah, reported the advance of the enemy from Martinsburg. General Johnston prepared to receive them, if they made their appearance; but General Patterson halted at Bunker Hill, nine miles distant. On 17th of July he suddenly moved to the left and occupied Smithfield. The Federal army now held a position which would enable it either to attack Winchester or to hold General Johnston in check, and prevent him from going to the relief of General Beauregard at Manassas Junction.

On the morning of the 18th of July, General Johnston was informed that the enemy were advancing upon Manassas from Alexandria, and he at once resolved to go to the assistance of General Beauregard. He had for some time understood the plans of the enemy, and had resolved upon his own course. His eagle eye had penetrated the secrets of the Federal commanders, and his fertile genius had prepared a plan for their destruction.

Leaving his sick at Winchester, he set out. Evading Patterson by the disposition of his cavalry, he passed through the Blue Ridge at Ashby's Gap, and moved towards Piedmont. The march was painful, and was performed under a burning July sun. The men suffered fearfully from the heat, and for want of water and provisions. They would even drink the muddy water from the ruts in the road. When they reached the Shenandoah they were heated and weary. But no time was to be lost, and they plunged in and forded the stream.

At last they reached Piedmont. Here the infantry were embarked on cars, and the artillery and cavalry ordered to continue the march. Jackson's, Bee's, and Bartow's Brigades were sent in advance.

While they are on the way, let me glance at Manassas, and the army there.

General Beauregard had not been idle. Naturally his position was one of great strength. About half way between the eastern spur of the Blue Ridge and the Potomac, below Alexandria, it commanded the whole country between so perfectly, that there was scarcely any possibility of its being turned. The right wing stretched off towards the Ocquaquon River, through a wooded country, which was made impassable by the felling of trees. To the left was a rolling table land, easily commanded from its successive elevations, until it reached an exceedingly rough and rugged country. The key to the whole position was the point which General Beauregard chose for his centre. This point he fortified so strongly that a small force was capable of holding it against one of much greater size. Nature herself had partly fortified it. It was a succession of hills, nearly equi-distant from each other. In front was a ravine, so deep, and so thickly wooded that it was impassable, save at two or three gorges, which a small force might defend against an army. To these natural advantages, General Beauregard had added every means of defence which his genius could devise, or his experience could suggest. Works had been erected at Manassas Junction, and other points, and a small, but heroic army collected under his command.

The enemy advanced from Alexandria, and halted at Centreville. By a brilliant retreat, General Beauregard withdrew his advanced troops within the lines of Bull Run, and led the enemy on to his position. On the 18th of July the enemy attempted to force a passage of Bull Run, at Blackburn's Ford, on the Confederate right, but were defeated with a heavy loss. As the battle of Bull Run is not connected with this narration it will not be described here.

The 19th of July was spent in burying the dead, who had fallen the day before.

General Johnston reached Manassas on the 20th of July, with Jackson's, Bee's and Bartow's Brigades.

That night, about eleven o'clock, Marshall was sent with a message to General Beauregard's headquarters. He found Generals Beauregard and Johnston in close consultation. General Beauregard recognized him, and shook hands with him, warmly:

"I am very glad to see you, Mr. Marshall, he said cordially. Then turning to General Johnston, he continued, "General, allow me to present to you Lieutenant Marshall, who was one of my Aids at Sumter, but who is now under your command."

General Johnston greeted the young man kindly, and asked him to what part of the army he belonged.

"I am an Aid to General Jackson," replied Marshall.

"Oh, yes," said General Johnston, "you are the man that shot Cadwallader's Aid at Falling Waters."

Then turning to General Beauregard, he related the incident to him.

"General," said Beauregard, addressing Johnston, "Evans has sent to me, asking for an officer to act as an Aid for him. From present appearances, I believe there will be warm work to-morrow, and a fine chance for distinction and promotion. If you and General Jackson are willing, and Lieutenant Marshall does not object, we will transfer him, for the occasion, to Evans. I want to give him a chance to show what he is made of. We'll give Jackson some one else for to-morrow.

General Johnston expressed his approval of General Beauregard's proposition, and the latter directed Marshall to obtain General Jackson's consent to the arrangement, and report to Colonel Evans at the Stone Bridge. He did as ordered, and being successful, rode over to the Stone Bridge and reported to Col. Evans. This was about twelve o'clock.

He found Col. Evans' little force lying upon their arms, resting and waiting the coming of the morn that was to usher in such scenes of strife. The moon was still in the Heavens, casting her mellow light over every object. Through the broken and undulating country, which was thickly wooded with clumps of trees, the narrow line of Bull Run swept gracefully on its way, its waters flashing like polished steel in the clear, cool moonlight. As far as his eye could reach, Marshall could see the gleam of musket and bayonet, telling that the brave defenders of the South were ready for the fray. To the rear, and a little to the right rose the gleam of the Southern camp fires. All was silent, save the rippling of the waters, and the hoarse challenges of the sentinels, as they paced their watchful rounds. Beyond the Run, the dark masses of woods rose sternly and solemnly to the view, with a dreadful and foreboding aspect. Above them the Heavens were lit up by a dull, red glare, which revealed the locality of the hostile army. Occasionally the deep boom of a distant gun broke upon the air, and then all was silent again.

Marshall gazed around him with feelings of awe and interest. No scene is more striking and awe-inspiring than an army resting in the silence of the night, on the eve of a great battle. Marshall could not sleep. He walked slowly to and fro, in the clear moonlight, thinking of what might be the result of the next day's battle. He trembled when he reflected what tremendous interests were staked upon it. The fate of the nation might be decided by the struggle. In that solemn hour he felt how weak are all human arms, and his thoughts turned to the God of battles, whose arm is ever lifted in behalf of the cause of right and justice. He paused in his walk, and kneeling upon the green sward, he bared his head and prayed. It was a touching and beautiful scene. One single man kneeling amid the armed hosts of Freedom, in the face of a powerful foe, with the moonbeams falling softly around his calm, upturned features, praying, in silence and alone, that the Lord Jehovah would go forth with the army to battle. And while he knelt there, far off, nearly at the opposite wing of the Southern lines, a man of noble stature and a lion heart, prayed for the same cause, and asked for that strength which on the red field of the morrow enabled him to stand "like a stonewall" in the path of the foe. Methinks that as those prayers rose softly upon the night breeze and entered the jasper portals of Heaven, a burst of angelic music gushed from the lyres of the Heavenly harpers, and the Angel legions of the King Eternal shouted for joy as they bared their protecting arms to strike for the freedom of an outraged land. Ah! who can tell how greatly the fate of the battle was decided by those two prayers?

When he had finished praying, Marshall rose, calm and strengthened, and walked over to where Colonel Evans and Major Wheat were standing by a camp fire reading an order.

"General Beauregard informs me," said the Colonel, turning to Marshall, " that the enemy will attack my position. So we shall have warm work to-morrow, Mr. Marshall. But excuse me," he added suddenly, " Let me make you acquainted with Major Wheat, Lieutenant Marshall."

The two gentlemen shook hands, warmly;

"By your name, I take you to be a brother Virginian, Lieutenant," said Major Wheat.

"Though I have been but a truant son, I am proud of the old State, and love her dearly. I am always glad to meet with any of her children."

Wheat was a large, splendid looking man, with a frank, open face, and chivalrous bearing. His romantic and eventful life had left its traces upon him. There was about him an air of manly generosity which at once won him friends. A kinder or a more chivalric nature was never given to any man than to Roberdeau Chatham Wheat. Kind friend, generous foe, may the turf rest lightly upon him. Let us deal gently with his faults. He loved his country; he died for her. Peace to his ashes.

Colonel Evans was a hearty, bluff looking man—every inch a soldier. His manner was sudden and abrupt, but he was warm and genial in his disposition. His keen eye grasped everything at once, and his fertile brain instantly devised some plan, which ever carried destruction and terror to the foe.

The officers continued to converse around the camp fire, and the night wore away. The moon went down and the darkness gathered thickly over all. Then the gray light of dawn broke the gloom in the East. Instantly the music of the reveille sounded along the lines, and then was heard the sharp rattle of the drums as they beat the long roll. It is a thrilling sound, that long roll, on the morning of a battle. How the heart beats and the breast thrills as it rings along the lines, summoning some to glory and some to the grave.

Marshall listened to it with eager interest. Major Wheat noticed this, and smiled quietly.

"The long roll seems to interest you, Mr. Marshall," he said. "Wait a few hours and you will hear more thrilling music than that. There is nothing that sounds so sweet to my ears as the roar of the guns."

He had heard it often under many a foreign sky. Poor fellow! it was the last earthly sound that fell upon his ears.

Soon the gloom broke away, and the sun of Manassas rose slowly in the Heavens. A few minutes after sunrise a wreath of white smoke rose from the woods opposite the Stone Bridge, and the heavy report of a cannon broke the stillness of the morning.

"That is their opening salute," said Major Wheat, his eyes brightening.

Col. Evans was watching the woods in front of his position. Suddenly a long line of skirmishers emerged from the trees, and advanced towards the Run.

"Major," said the Colonel, turning to Wheat, "throw forward one of your companies to hold these rascals in check. And you, Mr. Marshall," he added, addressing the young man, "tell Colonel Sloan to advance two companies of his regiment, to assist Major Wheat's men."

Marshall and Major Wheat moved off rapidly in different directions. As they did so, a Federal battery was advanced from the woods and a rapid fire opened upon the Confederates. At the same time the enemy's skirmishers advanced to the Run, and began a vigorous fire of small arms.

Marshall delivered his orders to Colonel Sloan, whose men were advanced simultaneously with Major Wheat's. They replied with spirit to the fire of the enemy, and held them in check.

As soon as the cannonade was begun at the Stone Bridge, it was taken up by the various Federal batteries along the line of Bull Run. The heaviest cannonade was directed against the Confederate centre and the right wing. The enemy wished to create the impression that those points would be most vigorously assailed. But watchful eyes were upon them, and master minds were prepared to thwart their movements.

The skirmishing at the Stone Bridge continued actively. About eight o'clock Col. Evans said to Marshall:

"Go to Colonel Sloan and tell him to leave four of his companies to hold the enemy in check, to draw off the rest quietly, and report to me here. Tell Major Wheat to draw in all of his men, form behind Colonel Sloan, and report to me here. Then ride to Gen. Cocke and tell him that I am convinced that the attack on my present front is only to deceive me, and that the real plan of the enemy is to attempt to turn my left flank, somewhere above here. Tell him that I have left a small force to check the Yankee skirmishers. I intend drawing off the rest of my men, and occupying a new position between the Carter house and the Brentsville road. When you have delivered these messages rejoin me at once. I shall need you."

Marshall delivered the orders to Colonel Sloan and Major Wheat, and then rode off to find General Cocke. He soon found him, and communicated to him the message with which he had been charged.

"Tell Colonel Evans," said the General, "that I approve his course, and will immediately inform General Beauregard of it. Tell him, also, that he is expected to defend his new position to the last extremity."

Marshall bowed and rode off. He hastened with all speed to rejoin

Colonel Evans, whom he found at the point to which he had removed. When he came up with him, he found the troops drawn up in line of battle. The left rested on the main (Brentsville) road, and was composed of the 4th South Carolina (Sloan's) Regiment, with one of Latham's guns posted on an eminence in its rear.

On the right Wheat's men were thrown forward, a little in advance of the 4th South Carolina, and Latham's other gun was in position on some high ground behind them. A copse of woods separated the two wings.

Colonel Evans was holding a consultation with Colonel Sloan and Major Wheat when Marshall arrived.

"We have chosen this position, and have determined to hold it, Mr. Marshall," he said, when he had heard General Cocke's message.

"They seem to be having a lively time on the right," said Colonel Sloan, as he listened to the thunder of the guns in the direction of Union Mills.

"That is only to deceive us," said Colonel Evans, calmly. "They will be here upon us in a short time."

Major Wheat sprang from his horse, and placing his ear to the ground, listened eagerly.

"What are you doing, Major?" asked Marshall.

Wheat did not reply, but continued to listen. Soon he rose, and turning to Colonel Evans, said, hurriedly:

"They are not far off, Colonel; and they are coming in large numbers."

Then addressing Marshall, he continued: "I was listening for the tramp of the enemy when you spoke. My ear rarely deceives me. I learned this from the Indians. We shall have warm work presently."

"To your posts, then, gentlemen," said Colonel Evans, as he extended his hand to each of them. "Remember, we must fall here, before we yield the position. We shall be reinforced presently. Farewell! and God speed you, gentlemen."

The two officers hastened to rejoin their commands. Marshall remained with Colonel Evans.

Major Wheat was right. The enemy were advancing along the road upon which Colonel Evans had taken his position. Having determined to turn the Confederate left flank, General McDowell had massed his troops in the woods around Centreville, on the night of 20th of July. On the next morning he moved forward two heavy columns, numbering in all sixteen thousand men, with more than twenty-four pieces of artillery. They moved by a road seldom used, and, making a long detour through the woods, reached the Sudley road, and crossed

Bull Run at the Sudley Ford, two miles above the Stone Bridge. To oppose this immense force, Colónel Evans could muster only nine hundred men and two small six pounders.

While the enemy are advancing, let us glance at a scene in another portion of the field.

At half past eight o'clock, Generals Johnston and Beauregard, accompanied by their *Aides*, dashed to the summit of a hill, overlooking Mitchell's Ford, from which they could observe the movements below them.

The day was bright and beautiful, scarcely a cloud obscuring the blue sky above. Far below the Southern Generals lay the plains which were in a few hours to be made glorious by a struggle fiercer than had ever been witnessed before in the New World. To the right lay the long dark lines of entrenchments, with their bristling guns, which had, as yet, given no reply to the deep mouthed thunder of the Federal cannon lying opposite them. Far away to the left stretched the broken and uneven ground occupied by the dauntless brigades of Evans and Cocke. Between the two armies wound the glittering line of Bull Run, with its wavelets dancing merrily in the sunlight. Beyond the Run heavy clouds of smoke hung over the left wing of the Federal army, hiding the hostile guns which hurled a storm of iron missiles upon the Confederate right and centre. To the right, the thick woods and undulating ground concealed that portion of their army from view.

With faces pale with stern resolve, and hearts fixed upon the Almighty God of Battles, the commanders of the little army of the South watched the scene before them. Shortly after nine o'clock heavy clouds of dust were seen rising in the distance, towards the North East. The enemy were approaching the left wing. Reinforcements were at once ordered to that point.

When General Johnston reached Manassas, it was known to General Beauregard that the enemy intended attacking him the next day. The position being too complicated to be learned in the short time at his disposal, General Johnston resolved to rely upon General Beauregard's knowledge of it, and to give his sanction to the plans of that officer. General Beauregard felt assured that the failure of the enemy to effect a passage of the Run at Blackburn's Ford on the 18th would prevent them from attempting to force his right wing; that the strength of his centre would render it safe; and that the real plan of the enemy would be to endeavor to turn his left flank at or above the Stone Bridge. In order to relieve his left, he proposed to advance his right wing and attack the enemy, while the left stood on the defensive.

This plan having received the sanction of General Johnston, orders were at once issued to carry it into effect. Thus matters stood when the advance of the enemy upon Evans' position was reported.

The day wore on and the Confederate Commanders anxiously awaited the attack of the enemy. Soon the booming of artillery and the sharp rattle of musketry told that the battle had begun upon the left. The designs of the enemy were now revealed. Soon afterwards General Beauregard was informed, that in consequence of the non-receipt of his orders by the brigade commanders on the right, his plan of battle had failed. He recalled the orders sent, and with General Johnston resolved to accept the battle as the enemy should offer it. Thus the battle was fought by them upon a plan forced upon them by the exigencies of the occasion, and which clearly demonstrated their right to their proud titles. Ordering fresh troops to be hurried forward to the scene of action, Generals Johnston and Beauregard at once set out for that point.

I must now return to Evans.

At a quarter to ten o'clock, a brigade of the Federal army appeared in front of Wheat's position, and only five hundred yards from it. This was Burnside's Brigade, in which was the celebrated 2nd Rhode Island Regiment, with its battery of six thirteen pounder rifle guns. Skirmishers were thrown forward, and the engagement opened. Wheat's two companies and the solitary six pounder kept up a vigorous and effective fire.

Just as the firing began, an Aid dashed furiously to Colonel Evans. His horse was covered with foam, and his clothes were thick with dust. He had ridden all the way from General Beauregard's headquarters at full speed. As he reached Colonel Evans, he reined in his horse.

"Colonel," he cried, hurriedly, "if you can hold your ground for an hour, you will be reinforced. General Bee is on his way to join you. I am going to hasten him."

Wheeling his horse, he was off with the speed with which he came.

"By Heavens!" cried Evans, as he gazed admiringly towards the position of the gallant Louisianians, whose deadly rifles were playing havoc among the Federal ranks, and whose "Tiger" yells were rising proudly on the air; "Wheat's men are heroes. Go to Colonel Sloan, Mr. Marshall, and order him to advance his men through the woods to Major Wheat's support. The six pounder must follow him."

Marshall hastened to the left and delivered the order. The men were awaiting impatiently, and as Colonel Sloan gave the order to advance, dashed through the woods with a cheer, and were soon at their new position. The firing now grew more rapid, for the battle had fairly begun.

It was a desperate struggle. Only eight companies of infantry and two pieces of artillery opposed to an entire brigade, and eight guns. But in spite of the fearful odds against them, there was no faltering among the little band of Southerners. Each man seemed inspired into a hero, and they fought with a firmness almost superhuman. History will cherish, and future ages honor the memories of that noble band who fought the first hour of Manassas.

Colonel Evans went everywhere, animating and urging on his men by his personal example.

During the engagement, Marshall was sent to the front with an order. On his return, he saw several of "the Tiger Battalion" carrying some one from the field. He sprang from his horse and approached them. It was Major Wheat. He had been severely wounded, but not fatally, and was being carried from the field.

"Gently boys, gently," murmured the gallant soldier, faintly.

"Major, are you badly hurt?" asked Marshall, pressing to his side. Wheat opened his eyes and recognized him.

"Very badly, I fear, Lieutenant," he said, faintly.

Then his eyes flashed, and raising his head, he exclaimed, with a feverish energy:

"Go, tell the boys to do their duty. Tell them they must not disgrace me."

"I will, sir," said Marshall, as he turned to go away.

"Thanks," murmured the Major, and he sank back exhausted. He had performed prodigies of valor, and had handled his men most skilfully, when he fell, shot through and through the body by a rifle ball. His wound was terrible, but, fortunately for his country, not fatal.

Marshall hastened back to the right. He rode fearlessly into the line of fire, and raising himself in his stirrups, shouted:

"Men, Major Wheat has fallen. He has sent me here to tell you to do your duty. He says you must not disgrace him."

The message was passed from man to man, and then there arose from the little band a yell of fury that chilled the young man's blood as he listened to it. Inspired by a stern determination to avenge the fate of their gallant commander, the men fought with a desperation that amazed and terrified their foes.

Marshall returned to Colonel Evans.

"Colonel," he exclaimed, as he reached him, "Major Wheat has fallen. He has been badly wounded."

"Poor fellow," exclaimed Evans, an expression of sorrow overclouding his fine features. Then he asked, anxiously, "Do his men know it?"

"Yes, sir," replied Marshall. They seem maddened to desperation by it.

"Good," exclaimed the Colonel. "Mr. Marshall," he added, calmly, "We shall be annihilated or driven back in half an hour. It is now a quarter to eleven, and we cannot stand this much longer. If Bee does not come up very soon, we shall be ruined. We can die here, but we cannot hold this position half an hour longer."

He had scarcely spoken when a tremendous cheer broke from the woods on his right; and a heavy fire was opened upon the Federal lines.

"Good," shouted Colonel Evans, enthusiastically. "Bee has come up, and we shall beat them yet."

At this moment an Aid rode up and informed Colonel Evans that General Bee had arrived, and explained to him the position of his troops.

Bee brought with him men worthy of aiding the almost exhausted heroes of the first hour of Manassas. With him came the 4th Alabama, the 2nd, and a portion of the 11th Mississippi regiments, these forming his own brigade, and the 7th and 8th Georgia, composing Colonel Bartow's brigade, and Imboden's light battery.

With the eye of a veteran he at once selected his position and brought his troops into action. Now the battle raged with fury. The burning July sun poured down fiercely upon them, but the dense wreaths of smoke darkened his light, and the earth shook under the heavy volleys of musketry and cannon.

An hour passed away and the enemy were being heavily reinforced. The Confederate force at this time consisted of but five regiments of infantry and eight pieces of artillery; while, sweeping down upon them, came fifteen thousand Federal troops and twenty guns.

It was a moment when the stoutest heart might have been appalled. Shot and shell tore through the ranks, man after man was shot down, but the heroes held their ground. The 8th Georgia, posted within one hundred yards of the enemy, suffered fearfully. The 4th Alabama, led by Bee himself, was nearly cut to pieces. The 7th Georgia and the Mississippians were paying dearly for their reckless gallantry. Evans' little band filled up with Roman firmness the gaps in their rapidly thinning ranks. Latham's and Imboden's gunners, the objects of a withering fire, lost many of their numbers.

But there was no faltering among them. The old classic war cry, "*Pro aris et focis,*" which ever welded into a phalanx of solid steel all the opposing elements of a Roman army, was ringing in each Southern soldier's heart, and nerving him to an iron endurance against the power of the foe. They thought of home, and loved ones whose prayers were at that very hour going up to God for them; for the bright and glorious land that had sent them forth to die for her; of a just God " who giveth not always the battle to the strong, but can save by many or by few;" and under the inspiration of such thoughts they resolved to die free, as they had lived. They would not, *they could not be conquered.*

Shortly before twelve o'clock, Marshall was sent to General Bee with a message from Colonel Evans. While with him, he heard him receive information that two strong divisions of the Federal army had crossed Bull Run and were endeavoring to outflank him. The message was hardly delivered, when it was reported by a courier that one of these divisions was nearly within musket range.

"We must fall back until we receive support," said General Bee. "Ride, gentlemen," he added to his Aids, "and give the order for the troops to fall back slowly to the Henry house." Marshall returned to Colonel Evans, and delivered the order.

The troops fell back slowly, and, at first, in good order. But the dense masses of the enemy surged heavily upon them and hurled a fierce and destructive fire into their ranks. It was more than mortals could endure, and those heroic regiments, which had fought so nobly, were thrown into confusion, and the retreat threatened to become a rout.

General Bee was riding with Colonels Evans and Bartow, in earnest consultation with them. Marshall saw the lines waver, and the troops sway confusedly to and fro.

Dashing up to General Bee, he cried, hurriedly:

"General! the army is becoming panic-stricken."

Bee glanced hurriedly around him.

"My God!" he cried, in a voice of anguish. "This must not be. Aid me, gentlemen, to restore order. We are not defeated."

Aided by his officers, the gallant General bent every energy to restore order among his troops.

Marshall rode along the line, shouting to them to rally.

"Form men! for God's sake," he cried, imploringly. "Think of your homes, your wives and little ones. You are fighting for them. Form, we are not defeated."

Suddenly the Henry house came in sight. This was the point that Bee wished to reach. Here he intended to make a fresh stand. Marshall trembled lest the army should not be sufficiently restored to form there;

At this moment his attention was attracted by a sight that he long remembered. Advancing rapidly across the plateau on which the Henry house is situated, a long line of men came on with the steadiness of veterans. Over them waved the Confederate flag, and another of a darker hue. He raised his glass, and gazed earnestly at it. It was the blue banner of Virginia. It was his own brigade. Jackson was coming to their assistance.

"Hurrah!" he shouted, as he waved his cap, enthusiastically. "Old Virginia to the rescue. Look yonder boys," he cried, turning to the men. "There comes Jackson. Rally now, and the victory is your own."

A wild cheer pealed along the lines, and the ranks closed up. The gallant "First Brigade" heard it as they came on, and answered it with a shout of triumph. Order was restored, and the enemy paused.

Bee and Jackson formed their men, and then the fearful struggle began again. The firing was kept up with increased fury. The enemy had been largely reinforced, and pressed the Southern lines heavily.

It was now noon. The small force of the Confederates was barely able to hold its position. There were signs of wavering. Marshall mentioned this to Colonel Evans.

"If we falter now, we are lost," said Evans, sternly. "But look yonder," he cried, pointing along the lines, while a tremendous cheer rose high above the roar of the battle. Marshall gazed in the direction indicated. What a sight met his view. Dashing to the front with the colors of the 4th Alabama flying by his side, General Johnston exposed himself to the storm of balls that swept thickly around him, and endeavored to keep the troops firm. He implored them to stand fast, and all would be well. Beauregard, with his noble features all aglow, paced his horse slowly up and down in front of the lines, holding his troops in check, and urging them to act like men.

These heroic examples were not lost. Wild and impulsive cheers greeted them. The troops forgot their sufferings. The broken ranks closed up.

"Colonel," exclaimed an old man in the ranks, addressing Evans, and brushing the tears from his eyes, "they can't whip us now."

At this moment a cry of horror rose in the direction of the Generals. Marshall gazed anxiously towards them. Beauregard could not be seen. Had he fallen? A moment of anxious suspense followed, and then a mighty shout arose on high, as the heroic commander sprang lightly from the ground. He was not touched. A shell had carried away his horse's head, but he had escaped unhurt. Mounting a fresh horse, he was again ready for duty.

General Johnston, yielding to the entreaties of General Beauregard, now left the field, and repaired to a neighboring point, from which he could direct the operations of the entire army. By his ready and skilful appreciation of General Beauregard's necessities, and his prompt and energetic action, he saved the victory then trembling in the balance.

General Beauregard now rode along the lines, and as he passed Evans' brigade, took off his hat and bowed profoundly to them. The men cheered him enthusiastically. Riding to Colonel Evans, he caught his hand, warmly.

"Colonel," he said, in a tone of deep emotion, "you have saved the army, and won immortality." Then, seeing Marshall, he held out his hand to him, which the young man seized eagerly. "I am glad to see that you are safe," said the General. "Colonel," he added, addressing Evans, "you can spare Mr. Marshall now, and I want another Aid. I shall take him with me."

"You will find him useful," said Evans. "He has been invaluable to me. He has acted like a hero. Good-bye, Mr. Marshall," he added, shaking hands warmly with him, "I hope to see you unhurt after the battle."

"I knew," said General Beauregard, as they rode off, turning with a smile to the young man, whose breast was heaving with proud emotion, "that I would hear a favorable account of you."

The two armies now occupied the plateau on which the Robinson and Henry houses are situated. The enemy's force had been increased to twenty thousand infantry and twenty-four pieces of artillery, and seven companies of regular cavalry; while the Southern army numbered about six thousand five hundred infantry, thirteen guns, and two companies of cavalry.

During the interval in which the events related above occurred, the artillery had not been idle. Opposed to the veteran regular artillery of the enemy, the Southern volunteer batteries acquitted themselves nobly. Stanard's, Imboden's, Alburtis', Walton's and Rogers' guns, alternating with each other in a rapid and vigorous fire, shattered and broke the ranks of the enemy.

The Federal ranks were now advanced, and in a few minutes came within half-musket range. A fatal fire now blazed along the Southern lines, and soon the torn and shattered lines of the enemy began to waver. Regiment after regiment was brought up to take the place of those thrown into confusion by the murderous fire, which, without a moment's cessation, swept through the Federal ranks. But each new regiment came up only that it might share the fate of the others.

On the enemy's right were posted the celebrated New York Fire Zouaves. The brilliant uniforms of this regiment made them a conspicuous mark, and being objects of special hatred to the Confederates, they had suffered fearfully.

An officer now rode up to General Beauregard.

"General," he exclaimed, "Colonel Stuart wishes to know if he may charge, and where he must go."

"Tell him to go where the fire is hottest," replied Beauregard, his features glowing with the genius of battle.

The officer rode off, and in a few minutes a wild shout rose in the direction in which he had disappeared. General Beauregard pointed towards the Zouaves, and all gazed in that direction. A squadron of cavalry was thundering down upon them. They charged right through the ranks of the Zouaves, sabering right and left. The red-legged ruffians broke in confusion, and the cavalry, sweeping around, dashed through them again and returned. Fresh troops were hurried to the assistance of the Zouaves. The battle raged furiously. The enemy made numerous attempts to outflank the Confederates, but were driven back each time by the terrible fire that greeted their advance. It was two o'clock, and it was evident that the battle could not be thus maintained much longer. General Beauregard gave the order for the whole line, (except the reserves,) to advance and recover the plateau. They moved forward with the steadiness of veterans. It was a grand sight, that bayonet charge. The enemy retired in confusion as they saw the long firm line of steel come on, and the plateau was won. The Federals rallied, and having received fresh reinforcements, advanced to recover their ground. Borne down by vastly superior numbers, the Confederates slowly fell back, and the enemy regained the plateau.

It was now three o'clock. Reinforcements ordered forward by General Johnston had arrived, and were posted at the needed points. Turning to his staff, General Beauregard gave orders for a general attack upon the Federal lines, and announced that he intended to lead it in person.

"Mr. Marshall," he said, turning to that gentleman, "order General Jackson to advance his brigade. Then ride to General Johnston's headquarters, explain our position, and ask him for reinforcements."

Marshall bowed, and gallopped away. When he reached General Jackson, he saw General Bee approaching. Jackson was wounded in the hand, but he sat on his horse, calm and unmoved amid the balls that were whistling around him. Marshall was received by him with kindness. He delivered his order just as Bee joined them.

Bee's men had fought nobly until only a handful of the brigade remained. Every field officer had fallen, and many of the company officers had been killed. Regiments were commanded by captains, and companies by sergeants, and the heroic few were about to give way.

As General Bee approached General Jackson, he exclaimed in a voice of anguish:

"General, they are beating us back."

Jackson's eyes flashed, the large nostrils dilated, and the firm, grave mouth grew more rigid. He turned to General Bee and replied, calmly:

"Sir, we'll give them the bayonet."

Then dashing to the head of his brigade, he thundered, "forward!" and the men sprang forward with a cheer.

General Bee now returned to his own brigade, and Marshall having to pass that way, accompanied him.

As he reached his men, Bee reined in his horse and pointed towards Jackson, who was dashing on splendidly.

"Look yonder," he shouted. "There is Jackson standing like a stone wall. Let us determine to die here and we will conquer. Follow me."

The appeal was irresistible. It was more than the hearts of the Alabamians and the Mississippians could endure. With a yell of defiance they sprang forward.

The whole line was sweeping down upon the enemy. The Federal infantry fell back in disorder. Ricketts' and Griffin's guns were captured and turned upon the bewildered foe, who were driven at all points from the plateau into the fields below.

The charge had been successful, but the success was dearly purchased. Bee, Bartow and Fisher, and a host of others, had paid for it with their lives.

As soon as General Bee had finished his address to his men, Marshall dashed off rapidly towards General Johnston's headquarters. It was about half-past three o'clock when he reached them, and delivered his message.

"My God!" cried General Johnston, in a voice of agony, "where am I to get reinforcements? Oh! for the four regiments I left behind me!"

His prayer was answered. Scarcely had he spoken when he was startled by a loud and thrilling cheer, which burst from his rear. He turned and gazed earnestly in the direction from which the cheer came.

"Have they outflanked us?" he muttered through his clenched teeth.

A dense cloud of dust rising darkly against the clear sky, revealed the approach of a large body of troops. They came nearer. The eagle eye of the Patriot General sought in vain to penetrate the cloud. Five minutes of painful suspense passed away, and his face grew as pale and as rigid as marble. Suddenly the head of the column came in sight. They were advancing at the double-quick step. Johnston's features grew paler, and he breathed painfully. A moment more, and a cry of joy broke from his lips. He had recognized them, and he shouted impulsively:

"Kirby Smith, by all the gods! Thank God for it."

Then tearing a leaf from a small blank book which he held in his hand, he wrote upon it hurriedly, and handing it to Marshall, he exclaimed, quickly:

"Ride, sir, for your life, and give this to General Smith. Read it on your way to him. Then return to General Beauregard, tell him that Smith is coming to his assistance, and repeat to him the contents of this paper."

Hastily saluting the Commander-in-Chief, Marshall dashed off. He reached General Smith, gave the order, and returning with speed to Gen'l Beauregard, repeated to him General Johnston's orders to General Smith.

Beauregard's eyes brightened.

"We shall whip them now," he said, joyfully.

General Johnston, in leaving General Smith at Piedmont, had ordered him to push on with all speed and meet him at Manassas the next day. But Smith was delayed, and did not arrive in the neighborhood of Manassas until the afternoon of the 21st. Here, for the first time, he heard, high above the rattle of the cars, the thunder of the guns. At once he knew that the great battle, so long expected, was going on, and that he was needed there. Hastily disembarking his men from the train, he pushed on at double-quick time, guided only by the roar of the battle. His arrival was indeed opportune.

As General Smith led his men into action, he was wounded and carried from the field, and the command devolved upon Colonel Elzey.

Early and Cocke had now come up, and General Beauregard gave the order for the final advance upon the enemy. The attack was hot and impetuous. Early's brigade had outflanked the enemy on the right, and now they were assailed in front and on their flank and in the rear. They fell back in confusion. Each moment their terror grew wilder. The rout had begun.

On, on swept the glittering line of Southern steel, driving the bewildered foe before it. Only a few hundred yards distant lay the sparkling waters of Bull Run, which the enemy had crossed so vauntingly in the morning. A fresh charge increased their panic, and breaking, they fled in the wildest confusion. The rout was complete. The right and centre of the Confederate army were advanced, and the pursuit became general.

Let us pause now and glance at a scene in another portion of the field.

Just as the rout began, a man of lofty stature, whose gray hair fell carelessly around his noble and striking features, rode out of Camp Pickens, surrounded by a group of officers and civilians. He was dressed in a suit of plain gray homespun, and a white slouched hat was placed carelessly upon his head. His eyes gleamed with pride as he listened to the cheers that rose in the distance, and then moistened with pity as he beheld the torn and mangled forms of the wounded, borne by him.

A man was carried by upon a litter. At a sign from the horseman, the bearers paused with their burden, and the riders checked their steeds. The stranger approached the litter, and bending forward, said in soft and gentle tones:

"My poor fellow, I am sorry to see you thus."

"Yes, yes," replied the sufferer, as he feebly opened his eyes, and fixed them upon the stranger; "they've done for me now; but my father's there yet! our army's there yet! our cause is there yet!" and then raising himself on his arm, he cried enthusiastically, while his pale face shone with an almost Heavenly glory, "and liberty's there yet."

He sank back exhausted, while the stranger's features seemed to catch the glory which was shed from the sufferer's countenance. One of the riders bent forward, and exclaimed impulsively:

"Look up, my friend, and receive your reward. It was the President himself that spoke to you."

The youth opened his eyes and fixed them eagerly upon the stranger. He raised himself on his arm, and gazed earnestly at him. Then sinking back, he murmured, with a happy smile:

"Yes! it is Jeff. Davis. God bless him!"

A shade passed over his features; the silver chord was loosed, and the brave young spirit had taken its flight.

Manly eyes were dim with tears, and there was a silence among the horsemen, as they turned their steeds towards the battle-field and rode rapidly away.

It was indeed the President, who had just arrived from Richmond, in time to witness the hard won victory of his countrymen, and the shameful flight of the enemy.

The shout of "Davis! Davis!" was passed from man to man as he rode on. The dying heard the cry as it pealed from a thousand lips, and feebly raised themselves to catch a last glimpse of their idolized President. Hundreds, who had been borne from the field wounded and exhausted, sprang up and rushed back with him.*

Let us return to the pursuit.

Just as the rout began, General Beauregard directed Marshall to go to Colonel Radford, who was in command of a regiment of Virginia cavalry and order him to charge the retreating enemy, and guide him to a point which he indicated. Marshall hastened on and soon found Colonel Radford, who was sitting on his horse at the head of his regiment. The men were all fine specimens of the sons of the Old Dominion, and were impatiently awaiting orders to join in the fray. Marshall delivered General Beauregard's order to Colonel Radford, who, turning to his men, shouted:

"Men! now is our time. Forward!"

Away they dashed at a full gallop. Marshall rode beside Colonel Radford, whose fine face was glowing with excitement. A cavalry charge was new to Marshall, and thrilling beyond description. Crossing Bull Run below the Stone Bridge, they made for the rear of the flying foe, while on all sides they heard the yells of the pursuers, the screams of the fugitives, and the thunder of the guns.

"Now the headlong pace grew faster,"

and away the horsemen thundered over the ditches, fences, brooks and trees. In a moment they were upon the flank of the enemy. A battery was passing at the time, supported by four regiments, covering the retreat of the Federal army. Upon this the regiment dashed, dividing in the charge. The infantry broke and fled in confusion, but the gunners stood firm. Unslinging their shot guns the cavalry opened a rapid and effective fire upon the enemy; and, then, drawing their sabres, dashed down indiscriminately upon them.

The troopers separated, some following the fugitives in their flight. Marshall now found himself with a small group of officers and men. The battery was preparing to open on them.

"Charge the guns!" he shouted.

---

* I have united two incidents. One related by **Captain McFarland**, of the Virginia cavalry—the other by President Davis.

The force was too small and they were compelled to retreat to their main body. As they did so, the guns opened on them.

Marshall fired his revolver at one of the men who was in the act of discharging a cannon. The fellow reeled and fell. Marshall bent low in the saddle, and the grape from the battery whistled over him. He reached the flank of the enemy and pausing, fired his revolver at the column which was passing him. He was now entirely separated from his friends, and he turned to ride back. Soon he came up with a Southern battery which was thundering on in pursuit of the enemy.

"Whose battery is this?" he shouted.

"Kemper's!" was the reply; and Captain Kemper at once rode up to him. Marshall told him who he was, and determined to accompany him.

"Very good, sir," said Captain Kemper. "I shall be glad to have you accompany me."*

They dashed on. Now the guns were unlimbered and the roads swept of the fugitives, who fled along them in the wildest terror. Now a Federal battery covered the retreat. Kemper's shells and solid shot were hurled upon it, dismounting guns, breaking carriages, and sweeping drivers and cannoniers from their horses and boxes. The cannoniers cut the traces, and mounting the horses, abandoned the guns and fled. Wagons were broken down, and the bridge over Cub Run was choked up with rubbish. The fords were blocked up, and the wildest confusion prevailed everywhere. Arms, clothing and equipments were scattered along the road and over the country; and the dead and wounded, together with those who had been overcome by exhaustion, lay thickly on every side. A dense mass of fugitives poured along the roads, through fields and over the hills, screaming frantically with rage and fright. Men were trampled under foot by the bewildered horsemen, who dashed into the throng at full speed. Those who were overtaken by the pursuers fell upon their knees and begged for mercy.

No language can describe, and no mind, save that of one who witnessed it, can comprehend the terrors of that terrible rout. A great army was disorganized, demoralized and ruined by it.

It was night, and the moon had risen, as Marshall, returning to General Beauregard's headquarters, passed over the battle-field. The moon was shining down in unclouded brilliancy, lighting up the field with a strange and solemn light. Men were lying on all sides, and in every conceivable position. The groans of the wounded rose fearfully

---

*The incidents of the charge are taken from the narrative of Captain McFarland, which is given in Mr. Pollard's History of the War.

upon the air, chilling the listener's blood. It is a fearful sight, a battle-field after the strife is over; and now the moonlight seemed to heighten all its horrors. Marshall had not been able, during the excitement of the day, to realize the terrors of the fight, but now as he looked back upon them he wondered that he should have escaped; and he uttered a prayer of thankfulness for his safety.

As he rode on he was attracted by the loud neighing of a horse. He rode up to the spot, and there beheld a sight that touched his heart.

An officer lay upon the ground, badly wounded. By him stood his faithful horse. The noble animal lowered his head and rubbed his mouth gently over the unfortunate man's body, and then raising his head uttered a loud and painful neigh. Then he lowered his head again, and the wounded man, raising his hand, gently and affectionately stroked his face.

Marshall dismounted, and approaching the wounded man, asked:

"Can I do anything for you, sir?"

"I am glad to see some one," said the officer gratefully. "I am not suffering much, but I am very thirsty. If you will place me on my horse, I think I can reach a hospital."

Marshall gave him some water from his canteen, and placed him on his horse. Then mounting his own, he rode by him, and supported him.

"This horse," said the officer, as they rode slowly along, "is a noble animal. He staid by my side after I was wounded, and seemed to suffer real pain at seeing me so helpless."

They soon reached a hospital, and Marshall having seen that the wounded man was properly cared for, rode off towards headquarters.

When he entered the room where General Beauregard was, he found the President, General Johnston, and a number of officers there, also. He advanced to General Beauregard.

"I became separated from Colonel Radford, lost my way, and stopped to help a wounded man, or I would have returned sooner, General," he said, in explanation of his long absence.

"Never mind," said Beauregard. "I am rejoiced to see you, for I feared that you had been hurt."

Then leading him to the President, he continued: "This is the officer of whom I was just speaking, Your Excellency. This is Lieutenant Marshall, President Davis."

The President held out his hand, warmly.

"I am glad to meet you, *Captain*," he said, kindly. "General Beauregard speaks highly of you."

"I am only a Lieutenant, Your Excellency," said Marshall, thinking that his title had been misunderstood.

"You are a Captain now," said the President, with a smile.

Marshall was confused by his unexpected promotion, and stammered out his thanks. The President interrupted him, and said, kindly:

"Never mind, Captain. 'Your modesty is equal to your bravery.'"

Marshall gazed around in a state of bewilderment. He saw the dark eyes of General Johnston bent upon him kindly. The General held out his hand to him:

"I congratulate you upon your promotion, Captain," he said, with one of his fascinating smiles. "You see now that General Beauregard was right last night. The left was the road to promotion."

"Captain," exclaimed General Beauregard, "you will remain upon my staff. You are now one of my regular Aides."

Marshall was overwhelmed by his good fortune. He retired into the group of officers, and received their congratulations. A hand was placed upon his shoulder, and looking up, he saw the grave, calm face of General Jackson. The General drew him aside, and said to him in a low tone

"I am very glad to hear of your promotion, though I am very sorry to lose you. I knew when I saw you praying at Harper's Ferry, that you would be successful. Continue to pray; it is the secret of all true success."

CHAPTER VII.

CAPTAIN Marshall's appointment upon General Beauregard's staff was very pleasant to him. His duties were not heavy, as the army lay motionless around Centreville. Early in August he obtained a short leave of absence, and went to Richmond on a visit. Here he met with Mr. and Mrs. Worthington and Mary. Charlie was in the 1st Maryland regiment, and he had seen him frequently. His visit was delightful. He was anxious to have his marriage with Mary celebrated before his return to the army.

"Wait, Edward, until we can see our way a little clearer," said the old gentleman, "and then you can have her."

In vain he urged Mr. Worthington to recall his decision, the old man was firm.

Soon news came that the army was advancing towards the Potomac, and Marshall hastened back. He found the advance of the army lying at Munson's, Mason's and Upton's hills. From these points the Federal Capitol could be seen in the distance, and the drums of the Federal camp heard. The gage of battle was boldly thrown down, but the "Young Napoleon" declined to take it up.

One day, while the army was lying at Munson's Hill, Marshall was passing a tent, when some one called him. It was a Surgeon with whom he was intimately acquainted.

"Come here, Captain," said the Surgeon. "There is a Yankee Major in this tent. He is dying, and he raves terribly. He has mentioned your name frequently. Come in and see if you know him."

Marshall was surprised at this, and entered the tent, which was used for hospital purposes.

On a low, rude pallet, he saw a large, fine-looking man, dressed in the uniform of a Federal Major. He was raving terribly, shouting and cursing at the top of his voice. Marshall bent over him. To his astonishment, he recognized in the wounded man, his old enemy, Captain, now Major Cameron.

"How came he here, Doctor?" he asked.

"He was wounded and captured in a skirmish last night," replied the Surgeon. "But who is he?"

"He is a Major Cameron," said Marshall. "I knew him when he was on Cadwallader's Staff. He is the man that locked me up in Fort McHenry. But poor fellow, I pity him now."

The dying man ceased his raving for a moment, and gazed at them. Marshall bent over him and asked:

"Do you know me, Major Cameron?"

Cameron gazed at him fiercely.

"Why do you come after me now?" he muttered. "I tell you I know nothing of her. She escaped. I know not where." Then raising himself on his arm, he shouted: "Drive faster—faster. Don't you see that hack coming after us. Ha! ha! it is down—broken—away—away. Ha! I have you, my lady bird, I have you now." Then he sank back, muttering: "Gone, gone. But that woman shall pay for it."

He was silent for a moment. Then he raised himself up with a great effort. His features trembled convulsively, and his eyes seemed starting from their sockets, he pointed tremblingly in the direction in which he was gazing, and muttered in a low, fearful tone that almost chilled his hearers' blood:

"Look! Look! Do you see her as she stands there? Oh! she is as beautiful as an angel; but there is an ugly wound in her breast. She is dying. Agnes, Agnes, pardon! pity! I was mad, I did not mean to kill you. Do not look so terribly at me."

He shrank back and covered his face with his hands, while he shook with the wildest terror. Then he sprang up to his full height, and struggled violently, as if trying to shake off some one.

"She has me in her power," he gasped. "She is dragging me down to hell. How the flames hiss and roar. Mercy," he shouted, frantically, "mercy, Agnes, mercy."

He fell back upon the bed, and his struggles grew fainter. Soon they ceased entirely, and he lay still and motionless. The Surgeon placed his hand upon his breast and then exclaimed, solemnly:

"He is dead."

"He has gone to receive his reward," said Marshall, as he passed out of the tent. "It was a fearful scene, and I trust that I may never see another like it."

Time passed away, and the army still lay at Munson's Hill.

One night Marshall was awakened by some one shaking him. Rousing himself, he found that it was General Beauregard.

"Get up and dress at once, Captain. I want you," said the General.

Marshall was soon ready, and accompanied Beauregard from the tent. They paused at the door, and the General directed him to watch the Heavens in the direction of the Federal camp. He did so, and in a few seconds saw a brilliant streak of light flash across the Heavens. This was followed by a similar light in another direction.

"What do those rockets mean, General?" he asked.

"That is just what I want to know," replied Beauregard, laughing. "I think there is some movement on foot, and I mean to play McClellan a trick. I want you to wake up Colonel Alexander, ride along the lines with him, and send up two dozen rockets at different points."

Marshall aroused Colonel Alexander, and delivered General Beauregard's instructions. They set out and soon fired their last rocket. The enemy's rockets disappeared, and nothing was seen of them during the night.

It was afterwards discovered that McClellan was advancing in heavy force upon the Confederate position, and that the rockets were thrown up from the different portions of his army as they moved off. When he saw the rockets going up from the Southern lines he supposed that his plans had been betrayed, and immediately abandoned the movement. His force was greatly superior to that of the Confederates, who might have experienced a severe loss but for the sagacity of their wily General.

On the 27th of September, Marshall rode over to Munson's Hill to carry an order from General Beauregard. While there, he noticed a number of men busily engaged in mounting a section of a stove pipe and a wooden churn upon the slight infantry breastworks which had been erected on the hill. He rode up to them, and asked:

"What are you doing?"

"Only mounting some Quakers to frighten the Yanks," replied one of the men, laughing. "We are going to fall back, and these will do to hold the enemy in check until we get away."

Marshall laughed heartily. It seemed supremely ridiculous.

That day the army fell back to Fairfax Court House, and finally to Centreville. The day after the army reached Centreville, Marshall rode to the camp of the Maryland regiment, to see Charlie Worthington. To his great astonishment, he found that his friend had been captured in a skirmish three days before. In a fortnight after this, he received a letter from Mary, telling him that her brother had been heard from. He was a prisoner in the Baltimore City Jail. Marshall's mind was at once made up. He determined to bring about his friend's escape from the Federal power. Charlie had aided him once, in a similar predicament, and he determined to assist him now. He informed General Beauregard of his plan, and asked his permission to execute it.

"I have some matters that I wish to arrange in Baltimore," said the General, "and I shall be glad to have them attended to by you."

Having obtained permission, Marshall at once set out. This was about the first of December. He had little difficulty in getting into Maryland, and soon reached Baltimore.

Here he learned that Charlie Worthington was in jail. He had been so open and defiant in his treason (?) that he had been confined in a separate cell. He resolved to visit him, and try to make some arrangements to effect his escape. In order to see him, it was necessary to obtain a pass from General Dix, the Federal Commander. This he resolved to do.

He found General Dix at his headquarters on Holliday street. He was sitting at a table, writing. Before he could state his business the General was called out of the room. Marshall glanced at the table, and on it saw two sheets of paper, signed "JOHN A. DIX, MAJOR GENERAL, COMMANDING DEPARTMENT OF ANNAPOLIS."

"I may need these," he said quietly, and taking them from the table, he placed them in the pocket of his great coat, and placed two blank sheets of paper in their stead. He had scarcely resumed his seat, when General Dix returned, followed by a clerk.

"Mr. Jones," said he, approaching the table, and resuming his seat, "here are the papers." He took up the sheets and glanced at them. "Stay," he exclaimed, laughing, "I neglected to sign them before I went out. Fill them up at once."

He affixed his signature to the papers and handed them to the clerk, who immediately left the room.

"Now, sir," said the General, turning to Marshall, "do you wish to see me?"

"I came, General," replied Marshall, "to request permission to visit an acquaintance, who is now paying the penalty of his folly."

"Who is he, and where is he confined?" asked the General.

"His name is Worthington. He is one of the rebel prisoners confined in the jail," replied Marshall.

"What is your name?" asked General Dix, gazing at him scrutinizingly.

"Henry Edwards," replied the young man, quietly.

"I do not know you, Mr. Edwards," said General Dix. "You may be a loyal citizen, but I have no proof of it. Are you known in Baltimore?"

"I am, sir," replied Marshall.

"Then bring me a note from some good Union man in the city, certifying to your loyalty, and I will grant you the permission that you desire. You had better come in the morning, as I shall go over to Washington this afternoon."

Marshall rose, and expressed his thanks for the offer.

"I have no particular business with him, General," he said. "But he is an old schoolmate, and I think I may be able to bring him over to the side of the Union."

"If all accounts be true," said General Dix, laughing, "you will have a difficult task. But you can try him. Good morning, sir."

Marshall left the room and returned to the house of a friend, with whom he was staying. Once alone in his room, he thought over a plan which he had formed while on his visit to General Dix. Then he drew forth the papers that he had brought with him. On the first he wrote as follows:

"HEADQUARTERS, DEPARTMENT OF ANNAPOLIS,
Baltimore, December 13th, 1861.

"Captain Henry Edwards, of the President's Staff, in compliance with a demand this day made upon me by the Secretary of War, is hereby ordered to remove from the City Jail the person of one Charles Worthington, a rebel prisoner, now confined there, and convey him to Washington, to be examined by the President. The Warden of the Jail will deliver the said prisoner to Captain Edwards, upon the authority of this order."

The other paper he filled up as follows:

"HEADQUARTERS, DEPARTMENT OF ANNAPOLIS,
Baltimore, December 13th, 1861.

"All persons are requested, and all officers and soldiers under my command, are hereby ordered to pass Henry Edwards and George Green at all times, and all places within this Department, unless specially ordered to the contrary. The above-mentioned parties are upon Government business."

Both of these papers bore the signature of "JOHN A. DIX, MAJOR GENERAL, &c."

"Now, General Dix," said Marshall, laughing, as he read the papers: "I think I can make a better use of these than you could have intended."

The gentleman at whose house Marshall was staying, was an intimate friend, and an ardent Southerner. Marshall revealed to him his plan, and asked him to go out and purchase for him a military cap and vest. This his friend did, and he donned them. About two o'clock Marshall took leave of his friend, and entering a hack, ordered the driver to carry him over to the Jail. He soon reached the place, and alighting from the carriage, and passing through the Warden's house, he entered the jail yard. As he was passing the window of one of the cells, he paused and glanced through it. He saw his friend seated upon a rough pallet, with his head resting upon his hands. His greatest fear had been that in his surprise, Charlie would recognize him and ruin the plot. Now he could prevent this. Taking out a piece of paper, he wrote on it rapidly with a pencil:

"I am here in disguise to rescue you. I have adopted a bold plan. Do not recognize me. Act your part as a defiant rebel.
"MARSHALL."

Then placing his mouth to the window, he called softly, "Charlie." The prisoner glanced up, and Marshall threw him the paper. He saw him pick it up and read it, and then he passed into the jail. As he entered the main hall, a large, florid-faced man rose and approached him.

"I wish to see Captain James, the Warden of the Jail," said Marshall to him.

"That is my name, sir," said the man politely.

"I have an order to carry a prisoner to Washington," said Marshall, drawing out a paper and handing it to him.

Captain James opened the paper, and read it carefully, and his manner grew more repectful to Marshall.

"This is a very strange order, Captain," he said, as he glanced at the young man, "but I suppose it's all right."

"Yes," replied Marshall. "General Dix goes over to Washington this afternoon. I am to meet him at the Depot with the prisoner."

"How do you intend carrying him to the Depot?" asked the Warden.

"I have a hack at the gate," replied Marshall.

"But Captain," he added, "General Dix tells me that he is very unruly, and advises me to handcuff him, to prevent his giving me any trouble. If he should attempt to escape, this will settle him."

He drew a finely finished Colt's pistol from his breast, as he spoke. James laughed, and turning to a Turnkey, told him to bring up young Worthington.

"Put a pair of bracelets on him first, Joe," he added.

The Turnkey disappeared, and the Warden asked Marshall what was wanted of the prisoner in Washington.

"I don't know," he replied, "but I heard the President say that he has in his possession information that we must obtain either by fair means or foul."

In a few minutes Charlie was led in by the Turnkey. He was coarsely dressed, and bore marks of the severity of his confinement. His wrists were manacled, and he walked along sullenly.

"Here he is, sir," said the Turnkey. "And this," he added, handing Marshall a small key, "unlocks his fetters."

"What do you want with me?" asked Charlie, gazing fiercely at Marshall.

"The President wants to see you, my snappish young rebel," said Marshall, mockingly.

"D—n the President," said Charlie, sullenly.

Marshall walked up to him firmly, and drawing his pistol, held it before him.

"Young man," said he, sternly, "my orders are to carry you to Washington, and I intend to do so. If you go quietly, you will be treated well. If you resist me, I shall blow your brains out."

Charlie's eyes sank, and he assumed an expression of dogged submission.

"By George!" cried the Warden, admiringly, "General Dix would like to see this. He has been trying for five weeks to do what you have done in five minutes."

"Come," said Marshall, "we must go. General Dix is waiting for us at the cars. Good-bye Captain," he added, shaking hands with the Warden.

"I shall keep the order as my authority for delivering the prisoner to you," said the Warden.

"Certainly," said Marshall, carelessly.

Then turning to Charlie, he seized him by the arm and led him roughly from the hall.

They passed through the yard and the Warden's house, and entered the hack. Marshall spoke but a single word to the driver as they entered it, "Barnum's," and they were soon whirling rapidly away from the jail. As they drove off, Marshall removed the fetters from Charlie's wrists, and threw them into the Falls, which they were then crossing. Then they broke into a long and hearty laugh.

"You played your part admirably, Marshall," said Charlie wiping his eyes. "But tell me all about the affair."

Marshall explained his plan to him.

"We are not out of danger yet, Charlie," he continued. "We have no time to lose. We must get across the river at once. We may, at any moment, be detected and pursued. The trick will certainly be discovered to-morrow, if not to-day, and we must get the start of our enemies."

In a few minutes they reached Barnum's. Under pretext of taking a bath, Charlie went into one of the bathing rooms and donned the plain black suit with which Marshall had provided him. Then leaving the hotel, they entered a new hack, and ordered the driver to carry them across the Long Bridge to Brooklyn. When they reached the bridge, the hack stopped, and a sentinel appeared at the door. Marshall produced the passport, with General Dix's signature, and handed it to him. The man opened it, and turning it upside down, glanced at it with a grave look, and then handing it back to Marshall, turned away with a satisfied air. The occupants of the hack could scarcely restrain their laughter at this little scene. The hack passed on, and soon reached the Anne Arundel side. They drove for a mile beyond Brooklyn, when they dismissed the hack, and pushed on on foot.

"We shall have to walk for ten miles," said Marshall. "After that we shall find friends, who will furnish us with horses."

They pressed on, and shortly after dark, reached a friend's house.

After they left the jail, the Warden paced up and down the hall musing upon the strange scene that had just occurred. He read and re-read the order which he held in his hand, until he knew every word by heart. Nearly an hour elapsed. Suddenly he paused.

"I don't half like what I have done," he said deprecatingly, "but I suppose it's all right. Anyhow, I'll ride down to the cars and see General Dix about it."

Mounting his horse, he proceeded to the Depot. He found General Dix sitting in a car, reading a paper. He approached him, and asked if Captain Edwards had arrived.

"Captain Edwards," exclaimed the General, in surprise. "Who is he?"

"The President's Aid that you sent to me for one of the prisoners," replied the Warden, slowly.

"There is no such officer on the President's Staff," said General Dix, completely bewildered. "I did not send to you for any prisoner. What do you mean, Captain James?"

"Isn't this your order?" asked the Warden, upon whose mind a new light began to dawn.

Dix took the paper, and as he read it, his face grew crimson with passion.

"Tricked by Heaven!" he shouted. "Captain James, that man stole this paper with my signature this morning. His real name is Edward Marshall, and he is an officer on Beauregard's Staff. My detectives have found out all about him, and are now on his track. You have been fooled, sir, and you must find these men."

The Warden was thunderstruck. The General glared at him furiously.

"You are a fine Warden," he thundered.

"But General, that is your signature," said James, pointing to the Federal Commander's own sign manual, which graced the bottom of the page.

Dix bit his lips with vexation.

"True," he muttered. "You were not so much to blame after all. That fellow was too sharp for us. Have the trains, boats and bridges watched, and if they have not yet left the city, we may catch them. I will be back in the morning."

Here the train moved off, and the conversation was interrupted. The Warden executed the General's order, and a rigid search was instituted, but no traces of the fugitives could be discovered.

Charlie and Marshall were provided with horses, and hastened towards the Potomac. On the third day they reached Saint Mary's county. They stopped at the residence of a friend.

The house was situated on the bank of the Potomac. A flight of stairs, almost concealed by the vines which overhung them, led to the water. Here a boat, with a sail and two pairs of oars, had been provided by their friend.

There was a third party at the house, who had been there for several days awaiting an opportunity to cross the Potomac. It was agreed that they should cross that night. During the afternoon, the host and his guest were seated around a bright fire, and Marshall was relating the particulars of Charlie's escape from the Baltimore Jail, when one of the gentlemen's little sons rushed in, crying:

"Father, the Yankee cavalry are coming."

All arose in alarm.

"Gentlemen," said the host, "you must cross the river at once. Go down to the boat, and push out from the shore, but lie under the bushes until the cavalry depart. If they see you crossing, it will get me into trouble."

They hurried down to the water's edge and entered the boat.

Scarcely had they left the house, when the enemy's cavalry arrived. They dismounted, and, rushing in, demanded the surrender of the Secessionists whom they said were concealed in the house. The owner of the mansion protested that there were no strangers there, but the Federals insisted upon searching the house. This they did, and finding no one, they departed, vowing vengeance against all "traitors" who might fall into their hands. When they had gone, the gentleman descended to the water.

"You must cross at once," he said, addressing the occupants of the boat. "It is not safe for you to remain here. Farewell, and may God speed you."

They returned the farewell, and pushed out into the stream. The river was about ten miles wide at this point, and a stiff breeze was blowing directly from the North. They set the sail, and were soon going merrily over the water. When they had gotten about three miles from the shore, they saw suddenly loom up from behind a point of land about four miles off, the dark hull of a Federal gun-boat.

"We are in for it now," muttered Marshall, through his clenched teeth, as he grasped the tiller with a firmer hand.

All eyes were bent anxiously upon the gun-boat. Suddenly a wreath of white smoke curled from her side, followed by a dull, booming report, and a shot fell into the water nearly a mile off.

"She has seen us, and is giving chase," cried Marshall. "Out with the oars, gentlemen, while I manage the sail. We have a long distance to go, but we have a fair start."

The oars were shipped, and four strong arms labored vigorously at them. The gunboat fired rapidly, and at each shot her range grew more accurate.

The wind freshened every minute, and soon it was blowing a perfect hurricane. The river was covered with foam and the waves were running quite high. The little boat flew swiftly over the water, now lying almost over on her side, and her sail bending and stretching to its utmost capacity.

An hour of fearful suspense passed away. The gunboat was gaining rapidly on the little vessel, firing as she came. The shore was fully a quarter of a mile distant, and the gunboat not a mile behind. Suddenly a shot crashed against the frail mast, literally splintering it, and the sail fell listlessly over the side. The crew of the gunboat waved their hats and cheered lustily. They now felt sure of their prize.

But the occupants of the boat had not been idle. Scarcely had the mast fallen, when it was seized and thrown overboard. The oars, which had been taken in, after the wind became so high, were now put out, and the little boat again moved towards the shore. The steamer gained rapidly upon them. In a few minutes she was in rifle range. Marshall now put out his oar to measure the depth of the water, and found that it would not reach his waist.

"We must wade ashore," he shouted to his companions, and suiting the action to the word, he sprang overboard, and commenced moving towards the shore. They followed his example, and abandoned the boat. The grape whistled over their heads, but they reached the shore. Here they waved their hats and gave a cheer of exultation, which was answered with a yell of fury from the crew of the gunboat. They then sprang up the bank and disappeared in the bushes.

Once in Virginia, they were soon enabled to reach their destinations. Charlie went to Richmond to see his parents, and the gentleman who had come over with them accompanied him, while Marshall returned to the army. He related his adventures to General Beauregard. The General laughed heartily when Marshall told him how he had fooled Dix, and congratulated him upon the success of his plan, and his safe return.

A few days after his return, Marshall accompanied General Beauregard in a reconnoisance of the enemy's position. They were riding slowly and cautiously along, having accomplished their objects, when General Beauregard suddenly exclaimed:

"Ride, gentlemen, for your lives. They have seen us."

All wheeled their horses and dashed off. As they did so, four field pieces were discharged from a clump of trees in which they had been concealed, not five hundred yards in front of them, and grape and cannister flew on all sides of the Confederate commander and his staff, who sped rapidly on. Marshall felt a sharp and sudden pain in the calf of his left leg. He leaned forward and clasped his horse around the neck. He knew that he was wounded, and he feared that he would not be able to remain on his horse. But holding fast to the neck of the noble animal, he managed to retain his seat.

At last the escort which General Beauregard had left behind him was reached. Marshall had only strength enough to check his horse, and then, exhausted by the loss of blood, reeled, and would have fallen to the ground, had not one of the men received him in his arms. He had fainted.

When he recovered his consciousness, he was lying in his quarters at Centreville. Several persons were standing by him, and among them was General Beauregard. A surgeon was sitting by him with his hand upon his pulse. Marshall opened his eyes, and gazed enquiringly around.

"Where am I?" he asked, feebly.

"In your own quarters," said General Beauregard, kindly. "You have been badly hurt in the leg by a grape shot. You are too weak to talk now. Come, gentlemen," he continued, "we had better retire. Captain Marshall needs rest."

They went out, leaving Marshall alone with the surgeon, who sat by him for some time, and told him that he must not talk, but must be still until he recovered some of his strength.

For the first week Marshall suffered intensely from his wound; but afterwards was more comfortable. General Beauregard visited him every day. He had conceived a warm friendship for the young man, and Marshall in his turn, fairly idolized the General. One day General Beauregard came to him and said:

"Captain, you are now well enough to be moved. I expect that you will be more comfortable in Richmond among your friends than here. I have granted you a furlough until you recover. I expect to be ordered to assume the command of the army of the Mississippi in a short time, and you can join me when you get well."

Marshall expressed his gratitude, and accepted the offer. The next day, which was the last of the year, he started for Richmond.

He was joyfully welcomed by Mary and her parents. Old Mr. Worthington had him carried to his house, and there he received the kindest attentions of his dearest friends. In a few weeks he was able to walk with the aid of crutches. The surgeon who attended him, informed him that he would never recover the entire use of his leg—that he was lame for life. This was a severe blow to him, for he had hoped to continue in his country's service. Now he must leave it. His career, which had opened so brilliantly, was now cut short.

One evening he was sitting by Mary, lamenting his misfortune, when the beautiful girl said gently:

"I am deeply pained by your misfortune, but I will try to make you so happy that you will not care for it."

"If you were my wife now," he exclaimed, enthusiastically, as he drew her to him, and gazed upon her lovely features, "I would not care for it."

"Then forget it at once," she murmured, gently, while her eyes filled with a tender light, and she gazed softly and timidly into his face. "I heard papa tell my mother to-day that he thought you had won me fairly, and that we might now be married as soon as we pleased."

Marshall caught her to his breast joyfully, and before he left her that evening, the wedding day was fixed.

Marshall wrote to General Beauregard, informing him of his surgeon's announcement and his approaching marriage.

In due time he received a letter from the General sympathizing with him in his affliction, congratulating him upon his good fortune, and assuring him of the General's unchanging friendship.

When Marshall was well enough to walk with the aid of a cane, there was a quiet marriage at Grace Church. The lovers were married without any parade or display, and returned home quietly, and soberly and discreetly entered upon their new life.

On the morning after his marriage, Marshall received a package from the President, and upon opening it, found that it contained a very flattering appointment under the Government, which the President tendered him "in return for his gallant services in the field." He accepted the position, and still retains it. He has not recovered from his lameness, and never will. But he is now happy in his own home, and in the society of his charming wife.

Mr. and Mrs. Worthington are still in Richmond, patiently awaiting the close of the war, when they can return to their home in old Maryland.

Charlie Worthington went through the glorious campaign in the Valley of Virginia under Jackson, and is now a Captain.

All parties are happy, and only pray for a just and honorable peace, when the country, for which they have sacrificed so much, and which they love so well, may take her place among the nations of the world, a free, a glorious and a prosperous nation.

May that time come quickly.

8

[Copyright Secured.]

www.ingramcontent.com/pod-product-compliance
Lightning Source LLC
Chambersburg PA
CBHW022148160426
43197CB00009B/1473